Repetition and Trauma
Toward a Teleonomic Theory of Psychoanalysis

Repetition and Trauma

Toward a Teleonomic Theory of Psychoanalysis

by
Max M. Stern

edited by
Liselotte Bendix Stern

with an introduction by
Fred M. Levin

Routledge
Taylor & Francis Group

LONDON AND NEW YORK

Copyright ©1988 by The Analytic Press
   All rights reserved. No part of this book may be reproduced in any form, by
   photostat, microform, retrieval system, or any other means without prior
   written permission of the publisher.

The Analytic Press

Distributed solely by

Lawrence Erlbaum Associates, Inc., Publishers

Published 2015 by Routledge
711 Third Avenue, New York, NY 10017
27 Church Road, Hove, East Sussex BN3 2FA, UK

First issued in paperback 2015

Routledge is an imprint of the Taylor and Francis Group, an informa business

Set in Palacio type by
by Lind Graphics, Woodcliff Lake, NJ

Library of Congress Cataloging-in-Publication Data
Stern, M.
   Repetition and trauma.

   Includes bibliographies and indexes.
   1. Psychic trauma. 2. Nightmares.
3. Dreams. 4. Developmental psychobiology. 5.
Freud, Sigmund, 1856- 1939. I. Stern, Liselotte Bendix. II. Title. [DNLM: 1. Human Development.
2. Psychoanalytic Theory. 3. Stress, Psychologi-
cal.WM 460 S8392r]
BF175.5.P75S74 1988   150.19′5   88-10395
ISBN 0-88163-073-X

ISBN 13: 978-1-138-87222-6 (pbk)
ISBN 13: 978-0-8816-3073-2 (hbk)

Table of Contents

Acknowledgments

I wish to express my gratitude to the following persons who aided me in the revision of the last draft of Dr. Stern's manuscript. Foremost, my thanks go to Mr. Nick Cariello, who restructured a sprawling work and laid out Dr. Stern's ideas with sensitive understanding; to Dr. Paul Stepansky, of The Analytic Press, whose constructive, critical comments after first reading the 1982 version enabled me to recognize the revisions that were needed. I also want to express my gratitude to the institutions and the librarians and staff of the institutions who extended their services to me so that I could complete the necessary bibliographic research: the librarians and staff of the New York Psychoanalytic Institute and Society; the late Phyllis Rubinton, formerly Librarian of the A. A. Brill Library of the New York Psychoanalytic Institute, who also permitted me to use the facilities of the Oskar

Diethelm Library of the Payne Whitney Psychiatric Clinic after she became head librarian there; her successor at the Brill Library, Ms. Ellen Gilbert. My special thanks to Ms. Jeanette Taylor, Assistant Librarian of the Brill Library, who not only met my bibliographic needs and obtained numerous interlibrary loans, but also lent a sympathetic ear to my many doubts in completing the project and also gave me moral support and encouragement; my thanks to my friends and colleagues in the biomedical libraries, who graciously allowed me to use their facilities when my search led me beyond the psychoanalytic literature. Thanks also to Mr. Gilbert J. Clausman, the former Librarian of New York University Medical Center, and Ms. Eleanor E. Pasmick, Associate Librarian, who kindly permitted me to read in the library and trusted me enough to let me roam the stacks freely; Mr. Eric Meyerhoff, formerly Director of the Samuel J. Wood Library at Cornell University Medical College, and his staff; Ms. Mary Mylenki, formerly Librarian at the Oskar Diethelm Library, Payne Whitney Psychiatric Clinic, and currently Associate Director of the Greater Northeast Regional Medical Library Center of the National Library of Medicine; Ms. Lee Mackler, Director of the Emil A. Gutheil Library at the Post Graduate Center for Mental Health. My thanks go also to my family and friends, who have been so patient and understanding in tolerating my preoccupation with completing this project. Most of all, my gratitude goes to my husband, the late Max M. Stern, who daily shared the thoughts expressed in this book with me and let me participate in his work, which so greatly expanded my horizons and allowed me the satisfaction of becoming a part of his life's work.

Editor's Preface

Shortly before his death in July 1982, Max M. Stern completed the last draft of a manuscript that represented his effort of some 25 years to investigate clinically and reformulate theoretically the correlation between biological and psychological processes in human behavior. In 18 previously published papers, he had argued that modern biological principles required just such a reformulation of classical psychoanalytic theory—not only the so-called metapsychology but the clinical theory—in terms of which psychoanalytic therapy was conducted. "Analysts," he wrote, "can no longer shy away from the task of reformulation and continue to cling to admittedly wrong postulates on the ground that 'psychoanalytic clinicians would find it very difficult to do without [them]' (Valenstein, 1968, p. 614)." At the same time, he recognized that *Repetition and Trauma* would leave "a host of questions still unanswered," and represented but the beginning of a process he hoped would stimulate further investigation and discussion by and between psychoanalytic and biological researchers. He understood, indeed, that his own effort might provoke the cry "Shoemaker, stick to your last!" To which he responded, "I can make no better apology than that offered by Schrödinger (1945, p. vii): 'Some of us should venture to embark on a synthesis of facts and theories, albeit with secondhand and incomplete knowledge of some of them—and at the risk of making fools of ourselves.' He concluded with Freud (1920): "Only believers, who demand that science shall be a substitute for the catechism they have given up, will blame an investigator for developing or even transforming his views" (p. 64).

Liselotte Bendix Stern

Author's Preface

Freud's prediction more than 60 years ago that progress in biology would "blow away the whole of our artificial structure of hypotheses" (1920, p. 60) has come true. As is well known, recent discoveries in neuropsychology have rendered obsolete the fundamental thesis of the classical theory of psychoanalysis according to which the motivation for all psychological processes is the need for discharge of instinctual energy. My aim in the present study is to examine trauma and repetition in the light of yet other recent discoveries with regard to the physiology of stress and the teleonomic character of the development of living beings.

In chapter 1, I consider the repetition of traumatic events in dreams in terms of Selye's (1950) conception of countershock and propose that pavor nocturnus be viewed as a physiological defense against stress resulting from a pre-

ceding nightmare. In making this case, I exploit the laboratory research on dreams conducted by Fisher and others in
the late 1960s. I depart from Fisher's *interpretation* of these
findings in chapter 2, where I suggest that Freud was indeed
correct in attributing such repetitive dreams to factors operating beyond the pleasure principle. These factors are examined in chapters 3 and 4, with reference to Freud's conception of mastery and my own view of "reparative mastery." In
chapter 5 I argue that such repetitive phenomena in dreams
and treatment must be reexamined in the light of Monod's
(1971) teleonomic theory of evolution if the psychoanalytic
conception of development is to remain consistent with the
findings of modern molecular biology. It is no accident, of
course, that the line of my argument thus follows closely
Freud's own in *Beyond the Pleasure Principle.* Like Freud, I
believe that a psychoanalytic theory of development must
ultimately be rooted in considerations of biology – "truly the
land of unlimited possibilities" (1920, p. 60).

Bibliography of Max M. Stern, M.D.

Anxiety, trauma and shock. *Psychoanalytic Quarterly*, 20:179–203 (1951).

Pavor nocturnus. *International Journal of Psycho-Analysis*, 32:302–309 (1951). Reprinted in: *The Year Book of Psychoanalysis*, 8:190–203 (1952).

Free painting as an auxiliary technique in psychoanalysis. In: *Specialized Techniques in Psychotherapy*, ed. Bychowski & Despert. New York: Basic Books, 1952, pp. 65–83.

Trauma, protective technique, and analytic profile. *Psychoanalytic Quarterly*, 22:221–252 (1953).

Trauma and symptom formation. *International Journal of Psycho-Analysis*, 34:202–218 (1953). Reprinted in: *The Neuroses and Their Treatments*, ed. E. Podolsky. New York: Philosophical Library, 1958.

Der biologische Aspekt der Übertragung (The sociological aspect of transference). *Der Psychologe (Psychologische Monatsschrift)*, 8:96–105 (1956).

Trauma, dependency, and transference. Presented at the Scientific Meeting of The New York Psychoanalytic Society, February 28, 1956. Abstracted in: *Psychoanalytic Quarterly*, 26:152–153 (1957).

Modern science and Freud's trauma theory. *Acta Medica Orientalia*, 15:183–188 (1956) (Jerusalem).

The ego aspect of transference. *International Journal of Psycho-Analysis*, 38:146–157 (1957).

Correspondence (with Moses Naftalin, M. D.). *Psychoanalytic Quarterly*, 27:630 (1958).

Hysterical spells. *Journal of the Hillside Hospital*, 8:162–174 (1959).

Remarks about an oral character disorder with blank hallucinations. Presented at the Scientific Session of The New York Psychoanalytic Society, January 12, 1960. Abstracted in: *Psychoanalytic Quarterly*, 29:452–454 (1960).

Blank hallucinations: Remarks about trauma and peripheral disturbance. *International Journal of Psycho-Analysis*, 42:205–215 (1961).

. Prototypes of defenses and defensive behavior. Presented at the 23rd International Psycho-Analytical Congress, Stockholm, July 1963, and at the Scientific Session of The Psychoanalytic Association of New York, November 18, 1963. Abstracted in: *International Journal of Psycho-Analysis*, 45:296–298 (1964); in Psychoanalytic Quarterly, 33:465–468 (1964); and in *Revue Française de Psychanalyse*, 31:485–486 (1967).

Ego psychology, myth and rite: Remarks about the relationship of the individual and the group. In: *The Psychoanalytic Study of Society*, Vol. 3, ed. Muensterberger & Axelrad. New York: International Universities Press, 1964, pp. 71–93.

Discussion of "Transference, Countertransference and Survival Reactions Following an Analyst's Heart Attack," by R. H. Little. *Psychoanalytic Forum*, 2:108–113 (1967).

Fear of death and neurosis. *Journal of the American Psychoanalytic Association*, 16:3–31 (1968).

Fear of death and trauma: Remarks about an addendum to psychoanalytic theory and technique. *International Journal of Psycho-Analysis*, 49:457–461 (1968).

Therapeutic playback, self objectification and the analytic process. *Journal of the American Psychoanalytic Association*, 18:562–598 (1970).

Biotrauma, fear of death and aggression. *International Journal of Psycho-Analysis*, 53:291–299 (1972).

Trauma, Todesangst und Furcht vor dem Tod in Psychoanalytischer Theorie und Praxis. *Psyche*, 26:901–928 (1972).

Death and the child. In: *The Child and Death*, ed. J. E. Schowalter, New York: Columbia University Press, 1983.

BOOK REVIEWS

Cooper, D., *The Death of a Family*. New York: Pantheon, 1970. In: *Psychoanalytic Quarterly*, 44:144–147 (1975).

Group for the Advancement of Psychiatry, Symposium #11, *Death and Dying: Attitudes of Patient and Doctor*. New York, 1965. In: *Psychoanalytic Quarterly*, 36:309–310 (1967).

Mitscherlich, A., ed., *Entfaltung der Psychoanalyse*. Stuttgart: Ernst Klett, 1956. In: *Psychoanalytic Quarterly*, 27:429–430 (1958).

Rheingold, J. C., *The Mother, Anxiety and Death: The Catastrophic Death Complex*. Boston: Little, Brown, 1967. In: *Psychoanalytic Quarterly*, 38:144–147 (1969).

POSTHUMOUS PUBLICATIONS

Death and the child. In: *The Child and Death*, ed. J. E. Schowalter, P. R. Patterson, M. Tallmer, A. H. Hutscher, S. V. Gullo & D. Peretz. New York: Columbia University Press, pp. 16–26, 1983.

Human behavior and the fear of death. In: *The Life-Threatened Elderly*, ed. M. Tallmer, E. R. Prichard, A. H. Kutscher, R. DeBellis, M. S. Hale & I. K. Goldberg. New York: Columbia University Press, 1984.

Repetition and Trauma

Toward a Teleonomic Theory of Psychoanalysis

Introduction

Fred M. Levin

I

Quoting Valenstein and Schrödinger to the effect that the greatest of life's failures is not to try, Max Stern ambitiously calls for the reformulation of psychoanalytic theory so as to take into account the progress in biology in general and neurobiology in particular. A clinical psychoanalysis grounded in the best knowledge of the brain offers our field an unsurpassed pathway for growth; for psychoanalysis to ignore such developments, however, is to risk losing status with the public, stagnating as a science, or both. Other specialists, not as psychologically informed as psychoanalysts, would then be free to play increasingly important roles in health care delivery systems. I am, therefore, extremely proud to have been asked to write an introduction to this volume and hope the reader appreciates the critical timeliness of the publication of Stern's pioneering attempt to integrate aspects of psychoanalysis and neurobiology.

Over five chapters, Stern lucidly reviews the growth of his reconceptualization of trauma from certain key clinical observations: of anxiety states and pavor nocturnus, of "traumatic" states, and of "regression" and "integration" within the psychoanalytic situation, where the fear of death is a prominent concern. At the core of Stern's effort is the challenge of integrating sleep research and dream research (see Gastaut and Broughton, 1965; Fisher, Byrne, Edwards, and Kahn, 1970). Reviewing these pioneering sleep laboratory studies, Stern uses their data to analyze the mystery of pavor nocturnus in adults and children. As I will attempt to show by introducing some of the work since Stern's own seminal studies, we are gaining new clinical insights into how sleep and dreams may relate to each other, and to learning. In essence, we are learning how learning occurs, what disrupts it, and how to correct problems in learning acquisition.

The panic, dread, paralysis, confusion, and amnesia of pavor nocturnus resemble, for Stern, the catatanoid state of shock of central nervous system origin (chapter one). Selye's classical work on shock points out how the brain is first aroused and then suppressed and even anesthetized by trauma. This effect is so substantial that surgery can be performed under its influence! It seems that the brain monitors the environment both outside and within the body with a view toward the early identification of threats, particularly those to the brain itself.

To assist the reader, let me add some general background. Kahn, Fisher and Edwards (1978) show that pavor nocturnus is a relatively rare phenomenon in adults, more common in children, and with rare exception it occurs only during stage IV sleep (occasionally during stage III) just as do enuresis and somnambulism. Gestaut and Broughton's (1965) view, as noted, is that these night terrors are not triggered by (NREM) mentation, that is, that the mental content in pavor nocturnus attacks comes after the unpleasant arousal. In contrast, Kahn, Fisher and Edwards (1970, p. 542) feel that a considerable amount of the vivid (NREM) dream content in pavor is indeed capturable, at least in some experimental subjects (more about this later). However, they are unable to confirm that the autonomic arousal events reliably precede the pavor attack itself. They are thus left with the puzzling conclusion that pavor nocturnus is preceded by a "physiological vacuum."

Stern concludes that pavor nocturnus represents "a defense against stress caused by threatening nightmares," a position challenged by some of Broughton's (1975) findings which Stern takes issue with and that seem to him disconfirmed by Fisher's later work (see pp. 54–55, esp. p. 52*ff*). He ultimately chooses two major foci for minute analysis: the agitation response and what he calls the catatonoid reaction, a form of catalepsy. The sequence in pavor is essentially that of a nightmare (in the preceding, stage IV sleep period) leading to an autonomic deficit, that is, the dreamer's reaction to his own thoughts is "an initial manifestation of shock" (p. 66). The nightmare, autonomic inhibition, and all the ensuing physiological shock reaction and defenses against this shock are then observed by the brain, are assigned meanings, and constitute the pavor nocturnus attack.

Vocalization occurs at the onset of the night terror, rather than at the end, where common sense might otherwise put it. It is this vocalization that the dreamer rapidly forgets. Rather than the scream or its mental contents leading to the physiological changes (heart pounding, sensation of rigid paralysis, immense pressure on the chest), the reverse seems true: these physiological changes are part of the shock and countershock that the brain is processing. That is, the brain both participates in and causes the (neurogenic component of the) shock reaction. The brain, in this sense, remains a not-so-silent witness to its own impending injury or even death, for along with the real (externally verifiable) scream, there is a kind of internal, paralyzed "scream," an emotional response to the potentially dangerous changes in pulse and respiratory rate.

The discussion in chapter two is, in my opinion, the most critical part of Stern's book. To clarify the discussion that follows, it will help to make some additional orienting remarks about pavor nocturnus and the unresolved controversies connected with it. To begin with, there is a tradition within psychoanalysis (and I believe Fisher's work, as noted, bears me out here) of seeing the dream state of pavor nocturnus as merely a special case of the regression that is generally exemplified by such things as dreams and symptoms. The core analytic idea is that during any such regression, the dreamer returns to previous points of fixation, presumably resulting from incompletely resolved conflicts at various developmental points. From this perspective the dream content (whatever is retrieved in pavor nocturnus) represents a by product of unconscious mental activity and can be analyzed as such (more about this later). What is controversial, however, regarding the special case of traumatic dreams is that no one yet knows for sure what their unique presentation signifies. For example, we are not sure to what extent mental content is really a factor in influencing what is traumatic about them. We are not absolutely sure either about the timing and significance of the autonomic changes that are associated with the phenomena (this is so especially because different investigators have obtained different data in this regard). Finally, we do not understand why some subjects have amnesia immediately for the mental content of the attack, whereas others do not (see Arkin, 1978, pp. 542–46 regarding these and other controversial points).

It may also help the reader to appreciate a second issue, related to but different from the issue of the dreamer's (or dream's) state of regression, namely, the dreamer's level along a developmental line. Stern pays attention to both issues when he considers dream and sleep phenomena as they concern pavor nocturnus. The point here is that not all dreamers are created equal: some have been arrested in their emotional development, and this fact in itself seems to be critical (usually undetermined in sleep research but more accessible in a psychoanalysis per se) in determining whether the product of their sleep will be nightmarish or not. Stern asserts, most cogently I believe, that "regression" during pavor nocturnus for the purpose of mastery over anxiety needs special qualification or elaboration if it is to be properly and fully understood. According to Stern, *the immature ego is incapable of dealing with severe conflict (trauma) without arresting its development.* He differs here decisively with Fisher, Byrne, Edwards, and Kahn (1970, p. 781), who suggest that stage IV nightmares are not dreams in the ordinary sense, but regressive phenomena with movements to earlier fixation points. Stern finds no evidence of "prearousal ego regression in stage IV sleep" dream material to explain sufficiently what happens clinically. According to Stern—who accepts Fisher's contrast between NREM and REM sleep and dreams—if Fisher were correct about regression, then experimental subjects waking up during stage IV nightmares would show some evidence of deeper or more primary process functioning, and subjects waking up during REM sleep should by comparison show shallower sleep. Actually the opposite is the case (pp. 71–72).

Rather than postulating a lack of ego regression, Stern posits "inadequate development" as the fundamental requirement for night terror attacks. Stern (p. 112) concludes at the end of chapter three that in night terrors *one is dealing with wishes arising ". . . in obedience to a compulsion to repeat, in the service of correcting a developmental failure to attribute meaning to a state of tension."* In the absence of proper assistance from the mother/caretaker, "dispositions will persist unchanged over time, as 'signals' of need to experience an external reality coordinated to an objective state of tension." It follows that *traumatic dreams are "not produced by psychic conflict." Rather, they can be traced back to arrests in psychological (ego) development resulting from a "lack of coordination with an original gratifying reality"* (italics added).

It is significant that such conclusions, although identical with some conclusions of self psychology (Tolpin and Kohut, 1980; M. Tolpin, 1983; P. Tolpin, 1983), have been drawn by Stern from a different set of assumptions, in particular from a lifetime of work attempting to understand trauma in terms of traumatic states, traumatic dreams, shock and countershock mechanisms, and from an abiding interest in integrating the observations and theories of psychoanalysis with those of the neurosciences. That both self psychology and Stern's research efforts have in this particular area reached the same conclusion (from quite different starting points) suggests that the conclusion is fundamentally correct.

In chapter two, after rejecting Fisher's position on the question of prearousal regression in stage IV sleep in person with pavor nocturnus attacks, Stern (pp. 76–77) agrees with Fisher's differentiation of REM versus NREM dream states: the "mental content of NREM sleep differs from that of REM sleep in being less lengthy, elaborate, bizarre, implausible, visual, and emotional, but more thoughtlike and conceptual in nature. . . ." Clearly, both Stern and Fisher recognize that during sleep something critical occurs within the brain, something that is reflected in dream and nondream states and that represents different aspects of cognitive/affective processing of emotionally meaningful experience. It is a tribute to the insight of both Stern and Fisher that very early they hit upon the importance of the REM/NREM distinction as relating to fundamentally different ways of processing information, a conception that has bridged sleep and dream research, just as it has stood the test of time.

In chapter three, Stern takes up the subject of trauma and the repetition compulsion. Night terror attacks "are . . . repetitive efforts to establish a beginning coordination between a state of tension and external reality . . ." (p. 113). He summarizes with a tidy dichotomy: NREM sleep "is devoted to the resolution of the . . . problem [of] attribution of meaning to one's own states of tension," which Stern sees as the central problem Freud tries to solve and explain in *Beyond the Pleasure Principle* (1920); REM phases "in contrast, would be concerned with the resolution of problems involving ambivalence, which would account for the greater appearance of primary process distortion in dream reports elicited from them" (p. 113). That is, for purposes of "defense" some distortion is expectable. In Stern's view, NREM ideation serves the function of mastery, and the repetition compulsion represents "mental activity more primitive and elementary than that associated with conflict" (p. 114). By this neat parsing of function, Stern has enabled us to imagine a psychological division of labor within the brain that fits with some of what is known about the organization of episodic versus semantic memory[1] between the two hemispheres (see Basch, 1983).

The final two chapters deal with a unitary conception in

---

[1]In an earlier paper (Levin and Vuckovich, 1983), writing on the subject of disavowal, I described the critical difference between "episodic" and "semantic" memory processes, the former based on personal memory and affectively charged feedback cycles, and the latter coinciding more with general knowledge or deductive thinking. My point was to relate these

the form of a "teleonomic principle" of biologic activity, a derivative of the thinking of the geneticist Monod. Human evolution is teleonomic, that is, goal directed, meaning that the genetic blueprint is paramount; thus all knowledge is acquired through learning programs that are themselves genetically determined and, one might add, species specific. From the perspective of learning, Stern might appear to be asserting that trauma asserts its effect primarily by inter- fering with the learning that ordinarily would have followed a genetically preprogrammed pattern, but that instead is aborted. For example, he describes a situation where trau- matically induced frustration during infancy or childhood leads to a disturbance in the "pleasure self" (p. 129) and to magical attempts to undo old frustrations.

Clearly, Stern does not make exactly the assertion just mentioned. I speculate that he "might appear to be assert- ing" such a generalization regarding trauma. In fact, I myself am raising this possibility, although I believe Stern's view is nearly the same. The justification for this hypothesis is that it focuses psychopathology upon a learning pathway that is vulnerable to biopsychosocial disturbances. In so doing, of course, I am not contesting the clinical usefulness of recent psychoanalytic studies of trauma, but only suggesting the usefulness (see for example Rothstein, 1986) of a novel, interdiscplinary approach (relying, for example, on learning theory), especially when one is otherwise left with a collec- tion of rather different and possibly fundamentally uninte-

---

psychological categories to the characteristic qualities of the two cerebral hemispheres, a line of thinking, supported as well by Basch (1983), that suggested to me that repression and disavowal might be defined as interhemispheric communication blocks in different directions. In a similar manner, if one keeps these distinctions and possibilities in mind, one can see that Stern's clinical theorizing leads inexorably to a view of dreaming as representing selective activity within various learning subsystems of the brain, including, of course, roles for each of the two cerebral hemispheres in REM and NREM dreaming. Later in this essay these points should become substantially clearer to the reader as they are elaborated.

gratable approaches. Although Rothstein's (1986) efforts in this area are exemplary, for example, they do not really solve a difficult clinical problem that requires some overarching theory.

To continue with Stern's reasoning, the reenactments that are at the core of the repetition compulsion occur under the primary effect of experience in the here and now. From my perspective, this essentially releases the "procedural" memories (versus declarative memories)[2] of the earliest (disturbed) sensorimotor schemata (see Levin and Vuckovich, 1987). Stern himself refers to this as "the emergence of . . . the primarily repressed" (pp. 129–130).

One may ask if Stern is correct in endorsing Monod's thinking of a "telenomic principle." My own sense is that to understand the human brain requires special consideration from a number of perspectives. For one, we have amazing brain plasticity,[3] even compared with related species. For

---

[2] Within psychology "declarative" and "procedural" memory systems have been described (see Squire, Cohen, and Nadel, 1982, and Squire, 1986). The former represent those memories which are best exemplified by learning at school. These would include learned rules, such as those for grammar or mathematics. Such "declarative" knowledge is usually retrievable merely by questioning the individual about particular rules. In contrast, "procedural" memories are not available to questioning, but need to be primed by experience within some related sensorimotor activity. This more like associating within an associative network; but entry into this kind of memory requires an experience, and what is retrieved is a display of the knowledge involved, which is proof that it was in memory in the first place. Such dichotomous memories clearly point to the existence of at least two, quite different learning-related systems. Actually, of course, the brain is made up of many such systems, and this subject is taken up in my previous efforts, as well as in the second part of this essay.

[3] By "plasticity" I am referring to the capacity to learn and grow emotionally, as reflected by the modifiability of the brain's anatomy (cytoarchetectonic details) or altered functioning of the modular systems of the cortex (Szentagothai, 1975) in response to experience. This subject is more fully discussed in Levin and Vuckovich (1987) and is of critical

another, we alone in the animal world have developed a material culture that contributes to our learning in ways that might not be predictable if one were to look exclusively from a biological perspective. The particular point of Monod's with which one might quarrel has to do with our being able to alter our genetic programming. Monod believes that this sets severe limitations; I am not so sure. Although Monod cannot be proven wrong categorically on this point, given the known capacity of the genome to alter its expressivity (McClintock, 1984) and our clinician's sense of human changeability, Monod's point seems exaggerated. Where one can agree wholeheartedly with Stern, however, is that given human neotony "the need for external assistance in the face of disorganizing states of tension" (p. 147) is absolutely essential. In this sense Stern seems correct in quoting Monod to the effect that a teleonomic principle does seem at work: trauma leads the human species to learn adapted behaviors that provide people, at times of psychological stress, with the necessary signaling and learning systems for obtaining help from others.

Stern, then, supports the concept of what has been referred to as selfobject functions (Kohut, 1971). He writes of the patient's state of tension, which is essentially mastered by someone other than the patient himself. For Stern no human is spared biotrauma in this sense, and our failure to master this "is at the very heart of mental disorder" (p. 118).

Finally, in chapter four Stern considers specific analytic case material, especially regarding perversion, feminine masochism, and compulsive personalities, all under the rubric of conflict psychology, as opposed to self psychology. For "fragmentation" anxiety, he substitutes the fear of death; in place of "grandiosity" of an archaic self, he refers to

---

importance in understanding learning, including learning in the psycho-analytic situation.

"demands for a magic formula" and "associations with Christ." This clinical material is written in an entirely unpolemical way, with clarity, intelligence, and compassion. One gains the impression of a seasoned and innovative analyst who has gone to unusual lengths to help traumatized analysands uncover new psychological capacities. For example, he helps these patients learn to use their own drawings and listen to tapes of their analytic hours to enhance their self-reflectiveness and introspection and to prime their memories.

The interested reader may well wish to spend time with Stern's articles, written over a number of decades. A review of Max Stern's work makes it obvious that he never hesitated to make bold leaps in attempting to explain difficult phenomena, such as the nearly universal fear that death holds for man. Stern returned over and over to this question with the insights regarding trauma and structuralization that I have discussed. Extending out from his consideration of pavor nocturnus, an early form of death angst that seems to be not uncommon in children although fairly rare in adults, are a number of related subjects that form a vital area of research today: panic attacks, phobias, catalepsy, shock and autonomic arousal, posttraumatic stress syndrome, and the general subject of biotrauma. Of course, Stern's major avenue of approach to this research was via his interest in sleep research and the closely connected subject of psychoanalytic dream research.

It has long been a goal of researchers to bridge sleep and dream research. There seem to be a number of paths along which such bridging appears to be possible. On the biological side, we now have (1) a variety of REM/NREM studies,[4]

---

[4] Throughout this essay, the dichotomy of REM versus NREM sleep is taken to be something the reader already understands. A few words may help some readers confirm the details of this understanding. Aserinsky

including developmental and evolutionary perspectives; (2) research on basic rest/activity cycles, circadian and ultradian biological rhythms, and entrainment phenomena; (3) studies correlating regional cerebral blood flow with a host of psychological variables and using a variety of noninvasive techniques; (4) research on brainstem mechanisms relating to pontine mechanisms or brainstem "gating" phenomena, and other system aspects between REM and REM-related changes in the brainstem and in other systems such as the forebrain, limbic system, and the like. On the psychological/psychoanalytic side is (1) work on dreaming in general; (2) research on "self-state" dreams in particular; (3) studies of the relationship between dream/sleep state, learning, and memory; and (4) studies of sleep/dream-related learning facilitation and inhibition (sometimes referred to as REM deprivation studies). These latter learning studies are extremely difficult to categorize since they have been conducted under an array of orientations: some conceptualize in terms of left–right hemispheric brain mechanisms, some in terms of the concept of brain "plasticity," and some from the

---

and Kleitman (1953) discovered the REM, or rapid eye movement, phenomenon in man, which seems to attend most but, importantly, not all of our dreaming. REM and NREM periods are specific phases of the sleep process. Sleep has been characterized (Tobler, 1984) behaviorally, electrophysiologically, and physiologically as follows: Behaviorally sleep has a typical body posture, physical quiescence, an elevated threshold for arousal, rapid rate reversability, and circadian rest-activity cycles; electrophysiologically, the electrooculogram shows periods of rapid eye movement five or six times each night (so-called REM, or "paradoxical" sleep), followed by periods during which the depth of sleep rises and falls (so-called NREM sleep, stages I through IV); the electromyogram shows progressive loss of muscletone, which loss becomes maximal during REM periods; and the EEG or brain wave shows low voltage, fast waves during REM periods, and high voltage, slow wave spindles during NREM periods. Finally, physiologically, throughout sleep there are periodic fluctuations in heart rate, respiration, body temperature, genital tomescence, and so forth.

perspective of the changing brain organization of large subsystems of the brain as a likely concomitant of so-called psychological development.

Given the complexity of the subject and the large number of possible approaches, I would now like to review some of what I consider to be useful work in the field of sleep/dream research, that is, work that seems to me to allow some significant bridging to occur. In doing so, I will try to be relevant and clarifying rather than comprehensive. In general, I will follow the major biological and psychological areas noted earlier.

I wish to state at the outset that Max Stern's work is the inspiration for the comments that follow.

II

Freud's *Interpretation of Dreams* (1900) was the beginning of scientific dream analysis. Subsequent psychoanalytic dream research of note (other than those research efforts mentioned in the first part of this essay) includes the contributions of French (1952) and Fromm (1947), who focused and extended dream interpretation within the Freudian tradition; Altman (1975), who summarizes Freud's lengthy and detailed dream treatise into one highly readable volume; Friedman and Fisher (1967), who relate basic rest and activities cycles of the brain to dreams; and Berger (1967), Greenberg (1970), Wasserman (1984), Gabel (1985), and Slap and Trunnell (1987), who have each made special clarifications regarding the task of bridging dream with sleep research.

The position of Freud regarding dreams, simply stated, is that when impulses and wishes from early, instinctual life (latent dream thoughts), and current experience (the day residue) resonate sufficiently with and reinforce each other, then one's latent dream thoughts are converted into a manifest dream by way of a process Freud referred to as dream work. This work involves a variety of mechanisms, including condensation, displacement, symbolization, and pictorial metaphor formation. Once produced, the hidden meanings of the dream continue to be protected from discovery by the continuation of defensive mechanisms. These include forgetting part or all of the dream, forgetting dreaming itself, secondary revision of the dream at the time it is remembered or retold, and even conscious withholding in relating the dream to others. The early stages of psychoanalysis were directed toward reversing these processes and getting at the unconscious sexual, aggressive, and other wishes thereby exposed.

Gabel (1985) contrasts Freud's view of dreams, for what they conceal, with Jung's view of dreams, for what they reveal of purposive, adaptive, and even "prospective" cognitive patterns. Gabel's inspiration comes from Montague Ullman (see Gabel, pp. 190–191), who, along with researchers such as Greenberg (1970), Berger (1967) and others, has formulated theories that seek to explain how dreams relate to such specific brain functions as sensory perception, the coding of experience, and the storage, retrieval and organization of memory.

Before I continue, however, I would like to note some important issues. One is the problem of dealing with the information-processing aspects of dreams without shifting the focus so as to destroy the meaning of dreams as described by Freud, which has proven monumentally important in clinical psychoanalysis. In addition, we also do not want to gloss over the differences between Freud and Jung, which are considerable and which add another problem of deciding how to consider the possible meanings of any particular dream. Finally, in any synthesis we want to bridge the humanistic and scientific traditions represented within each relevant theoretical approach.

To begin, it is clear that Freud unequivocally rejected Jung's views on dreams. For example, he writes (1916/1917) of some psychoanalysts who erroneously assert

> that dreams are concerned with attempts at adaptation to present conditions and with attempts at solving future problems—that they have a "prospective purpose". . . . We have already shown [however] that this assertion is based upon a confusion between the [manifest] dream and the latent dream thoughts and is therefore based on disregarding the dream-work. As a characterization of the unconscious intellectual activity of which the latent dream thoughts form part, it is on the one hand no novelty and on the other not exhaustive, since unconsious intellectual activity is occupied with many other things besides preparing for the future [pp. 236–237].

Further, Jung seems no less to have rejected Freud's views on dreams. In particular, Jung rejected Freud's sense of the critical importance that dreams hold for gaining access to hidden sexual and aggressive impulses, which according to Freud is at the core of dreams as well as the psychopathology of everyday life. To Jung, sexual and aggressive motives are part of life, but substantially less important than such other issues as "individuation" (Henderson and Wheelwright, 1974, p. 817) and "the inherited structure of the brain," which Jung referred to as the "collective unconscious" (p. 809).

Because of this historic controversy it is possible to read various statements that seek to bridge dream and sleep research as fundamentally continuing the controversy in some polemical manner. This is something I wish to avoid, as much as is possible. I hope this can be accomplished by focusing more upon dream and sleep phenomena per se and as they relate to each other and less on what is implied about fundamental human nature.

Beginning with some of the early work on dreams and sleep, Greenberg states that

> the dream process serves to bring together percep-tions of recent emotionally meaningful experiences with memories of past experiences of a similar nature . . . the new experiences can be dealt with in the same manner as the earlier experiences, or the new experi-ences might indicate that the earlier experiences no longer need to be handled with the hold, characteristic but outmoded methods of adaptation. This latter event can be seen as effecting a change in the memory system rather than just adding new information to it [Greenberg, 1970, p. 265].

Greenberg (1970) credits Dewan with the idea that memory filing seems most likely to be "according to emotional tone" (p. 265; also see Dewan, 1970). Greenberg also cites still earlier research by Pariagiani and Zannocco in 1963 and Passouant and Cadhilac in 1962 for showing that "hippo-campal activation [occurs] during paradoxical [i.e. REM] sleep in cats" (pp. 259–260). Importantly, this kind of hippo-campal theta activation has been related by Meissner (1966) to learning and memory processing in animals.

In his early work, Berger (1970) clarifies that REM sleep serves multiple functions, a finding which the literature continues to confirm. These functions include maintaining "the integrity of the CNS process involved in the coordina-tion of eye movement, which coordination would be lost if there were extended periods of sleep without periodic [REM sleep] enervation of the oculomotor system" (pp. 278). According to Berger, Dewan feels that the key in all of this is that the REM "reprogramming" occurs offline, that is, during sleep (p. 296). It thus gives the organism a chance to gain in efficiency during the day by saving information for processing later on, thus relieving the organism of the need to both perceive and process information simultaneously. This idea is later reintroduced by Winson (1985) in reviewing the subject of dream and sleep research.

One cannot review this research without commenting, if only briefly, on the technologies involved. Several methodologies have provided information about selective information processing in man. Since the 1960s it has been known that the brain generates electrical potentials in relation to high level cognitive operations (Desmedt, 1979). Unfortunately, "the problem involved in obtaining valid correlations between [such variables as] ERP [evoked response potential] components and selective processes in man are formidable" (Hillyard, 1979, p. 9); also, the focus until now has been to study subjects who are awake, where the cognitive task and evoked potential response can more easily be related to each other. There apparently is very little that exploits this technique to understand fundamentally the information system activity during dreaming. In addition, from approximately the same time period, regional cerebral blood flow studies (see Lassen, 1987, for a review of research in this field; also Roland and Friberg, 1985, and Friberg and Roland, 1987) have provided further clues regarding complex brain information processing during the waking state. Again, to my knowledge nothing has been done on sleeping subjects.

What is important here, however, is that unlike the electrical studies, CAT scans, and NMR techniques that are available, the radioactive xenon scanning techniques of Lassen and other researchers for following regional cerebral

blood flow seem potentially the most valuable for the ultimate bridging of sleep and dream research. This is because,
unlike some of the other tests (particularly CAT scanning
and NMR), they are supremely functional, that is, they show
us what the brain is doing. (PET scanning is too expensive
and too infrequently done to be of much practical value.) It is
unfortunate that we have already spent scarce funds for such
expensive equipment when it is not likely to help us learn
what is going on (for example, during sleep) in the deeper
structures of the brain. When more Xenon scanning ma-
chines are available (of the latest type developed by Lassen)
and studies have been extended to sleeping subjects, we
shall have our first detailed insights into what the processing
patterns are between and within deep and surface brain
structures during the sleeping state. We will then be able to
test out some of the hypotheses that attempt to integrate
dream and sleep phenomena.

But there is another reason for the lack of progress in
bridging dream and sleep research. Unfortunately, while
psychoanalysts and others have been trying to understand
the research on REM sleep, a number of brain scientists, not
satisfied with simply making discoveries in their own field,
have chosen to criticize psychoanalytic dream theory. This
has led to articles like Wasserman's (1984) and Rechtschaffen's (1983), which point out the faults in such criticism as
that from Hobson and McCarley (1977). The problem is that
this effort to defend psychoanalysis from unwarranted criticism has required time and effort that would better have
been spent in reviewing REM research findings, evaluating
the evidence, and integrating insights with what is being
accomplished within psychoanalytically oriented dream research.

A third reason for the failure in effecting the bridge is
the failure of psychoanalysis to appreciate some of its own
dream research. An important area of this research has been

so-called self-state dreams, a designation attributed falsely to Kohut in a psychoanalytic article by Slap and Trunnell (1987). In fact, self-state dreams seem to have been part of Jung's contribution to psychiatry (see Gabel, 1985), and although Kohut and others (Tolpin and Kohut, 1980; P. Tolpin, 1983; M. Tolpin, 1983) deserve credit for rescuing this insight, I do not believe they initiated it. Moreover, although Kohut did discuss such dreams, he did not introduce the subject in 1977, as indicated by Slapp and Trunnell (p. 252), but in 1971, in *The Analysis of the Self*. My intention here, however, is not to find fault with scholarly psychoanalytic articles. Rather it is to rescue the important concept of self-state dreams, which might otherwise be buried within self psychology and forgotten. There is an unfortunate tendency to praise overmuch certain theories when they are new and to discard their hard-won insights when they become subject to criticism. I think this is exactly what has happened with self-state dreams. In what follows, however, I will try to demonstrate that Jung's insights, along with Kohut's (and the Tolpins') *regarding this aspect of dream interpretation* are extemely important to clinical practice and that they are not necessarily at variance with the sound practice of psychoanalysis according to a conflict model. There is no reason, in other words, why dreams cannot be examined from both conflict and nonconflict perspectives, just as Max Stern has done, to see which is more apt in a particular case or whether or not both views might prevail. In fact, we have in psychoanalysis ample precedent for doing exactly this in Freud's use of the genetic, adaptive, topographic, and other psychoanalytic viewpoints, more or less simultaneously.

Now, what is particularly interesting about the self-state dream, in my opinion, is that there is now an abundance of information in neuroscience that relates to how experience is perceived, stored, organized, and retrieved; and this new scientific study of learning as a process has a very great bearing on the learning blocks that occur in persons who identify themselves as in need of psychiatric help (see Levin and Vuckovich, 1987). In fact, *it may be the recognition by the experiencing self of the very existence of those learning blocks and the dangers they represent that self-state dreams announce.* And when such dangers pass some critical threshold, so that external help is needed, then we have a nightmare instead of a dream. If these speculations prove correct, then we must make use of all that we know psychoanalytically *and* neurologically to better understand our analysands. This would mean properly decoding the self-related danger in such traumatic dreams.

My thinking about this integration (and what I am about to speculate about) has crystalized over years and has grown from the daily attempt to understand dreams with my patients, either in psychotherapy or psychoanalysis. It also flows from a lifelong interest in the brain and how it works, although my formal research in integrating psychoanalytic and neuroscience perspectives really started in 1971, when I began my residency in psychiatry under Roy Grinker, Sr., who will, for me, always be the best example of a disciplined scholar of the mind and brain. During my training I also had the opportunity to study with Michael Basch and to meet briefly but significantly with Ludwig von Bertalanffy, the father of general systems theory. Both had a profound effect upon my thinking.

I would like to try to describe now the synthesis I have made, leaving the bulk of the details for the third section of this introduction. This will make it easier for the reader to understand what follows, as well as making it easier for me to direct my own thinking in a highly complex area. My thinking begins with the following ideas. Sleeping is not really necessary for life but is an expression of an evolutionary trend in brain development, that is, of the particular pathway through which our particular kind of (human) brain came into being (see Tobler, 1984). In the same way, even the other life forms that sleep do not all have REM/NREM cycles built into them: Thus, some animals do not sleep, and others sleep in a different way than we do. For example, low voltage, fast-wave sleep (i.e. REM sleep) is absent in fish and amphibians, questionable in reptiles, and definitely present in birds and marsupials (p. 215). Yet if one looks at the EEG for differences between vigilance states, one can definitely find these present in reptiles and even some fish. Thus, as we move up the evolutionary ladder, we come to life forms that sleep with REM and NREM periods as an important pattern whose brains are organized in this way for a purpose that is both discoverable and adaptive. I feel that the person who has come closest to discovering this purpose is Dewan (1970) who speculated about the efficiency of offline processing. I think we can now specify even more about exactly what this means.

My main points concern what specifically the organizational changes consist of when, during alternating periods of REM and NREM sleep, something is occurring that is critical for learning. My impression is that the organizational changes occurring in the brain during sleep relate to the following specific system relationships and confer some adaptive value, such as planning for biopsychosocial realities. (1) There are at least three major learning-adapted systems of the brain, and these, *during REM periods, repeatedly "review" the day's residue*, which they have individually received during the subject's recent experiencing: This review is possible because, during the REM periods, critical learning systems or their parts are relatively separated from each other (see Bakan, 1978). By "review" I mean the creation of a long-term memory storage form for particular memories, which were previously in some intermediate form. I also assume that a critical step in this process involves some final rearrangements in the organization of these memories, for example, according to affect (see Dewan, 1970). (2) These three systems are the vestibulocerebellar system (VCS), the corticostriatal system (CSS), and the corticolimbic system (CLS), each of which could be related to a particular category of knowledge and orientation, which I will discuss presently. (3) Each of these three systems, in my opinion, has its own vocabulary and unique "perspective," which differ to some degree from the others. One of the next necessary tasks in information processing might be the communication of these three great systems with each other, *downloading,* which I believe *occurs primarily during the NREM periods* (when these major information-processing systems are connected). That is, each of these three systems is outputting and inputting its load of information into or from the other two systems during NREM periods. This downloading must result in further learning for each system, since each receiving system will have loading for the same "event" but from no less than three quite different "perspectives." I further assume that these processes of review and downloading are connected to each other, or interdependent, and that this explains the need for alternating REM with NREM periods. (4) The effect of this sharing of information evidently is to update the primary database within each system, and with this, each system probably can begin to have some emotional or other reaction to this exchange. Specifically, the potential reactions seem likely to include as well the patterns earlier described by Stern for REM and NREM sleep (p. 5 of this essay). (5) In my opinion, the system relationships between these three major learning systems are critical. It is also possible that the smoothness or lack of integration or cohesion within the overall operating system that we call brain is very much effected by how well these three subsystems work with each other. In a parallel way, I have discussed elsewhere (Levin and Vuckovich, 1983) how the two cerebral hemispheres can either collaborate or conflict, with potentially serious effects on the overall personality functioning. (6) This means that we can consider the dream not only as a reflection of the CLS, as I believe Freud did, in what we call the conflict-psychological perspective, but as reflective of nonconflict-based issues, indicating, I believe, the functioning of the two other systems as well, the CSS and the VCS. To my mind, these two additional systems are primarily concerned with the status of the prerepresentational self (see Emde, 1983) and are designed to accomplish a different set of tasks than the CLS. In fact, what have been called self-state dreams, may be reports of the status of these latter two systems, particularly when these systems register a condition of danger to the self (as occurs in nightmares, but is not restricted to such traumatic dreams).

I have considerably extended the number of assertions and questions that must be answered. At least, however, I have laid the ground work for filling in some of the details; I have also introduced the possibility that these issues of brain function (learning subsystems) and dream state might profitably be related to each other. And I have given us some clues to how we might proceed with the necessary clarifications.

One clarification that can be made at the outset concerns what I meant when I said that each of the three major learning systems is connected with a particular traditional domain or viewpoint. Let me explain. The CLS represents the traditional psychoanalytic perspective in particular, but also the psychological sphere in general, since it is concerned with integrating the great limbic system (and therefore our right-hemispheric, affect-regulation system) and that which we learn through society (the left-hemispheric language and cultural, rule-related system). In psychoanalysis, as it was begun by its founder, the issue was of integrating these two opposing hemispheric perspectives that placed the person with sexual or aggressive instincts/drives in the problem situation of dealing with particular cultural prohibitions.

In contrast to the CLS [or CLDS, for corticolimbic

diencephalic system], the VCS represents the leading edge of the biological sphere: it relates more to the establishment of a core sense of self, or the self-in-the-world model (see Levin and Vuckovich, 1987). Fricke (1982), in a particularly valuable contribution, relates the development of this particular system to the establishment of the ego (or, one might say, the self). To my mind, this learning system, available since birth (see Levin, 1987), is the biological basis for the establishment of the prerepresentational self (see Emde, 1983). Trevarthen (1979, 1985) has also pointed out the complexities involved in specifying which neuroanatomical structures might be involved in developmental steps; and although he might disagree with the particulars suggested herein, I think he would agree with the spirit of this enterprise, namely, that it is worthwhile to begin to think about what brain systems and what behavior are related to each other. The VCS, then, explains some of the functions observed in early child observation studies, whether psychological or preoedipally psychoanalytic.

The third system, the CSS, represents the leading edge of the social sphere insofar as it is an excellent system for acquiring habit patterns, and these are the building blocks of social roles. This system has been ably described by Mishkin, Malamut, and Bechevalier (1984) and refers, again, to a system that (in contrast to the CLS, which requires years for its maturation and numerous experiences for its registry) is available from birth and often requires only a single sensory experience for the learning to occur! Young children use the CSS function as competently as adults. This system explains the data accumulated over years by those in academic psychology and other specialties that relate to the acquisition of habits (versus more complex memories, such as are acquired through discriminative learning).

Of course, another obvious reason for paying attention to the differences in the functioning of these three different systems is that armed with this perspective one can avoid getting caught up in needless debates over what learning is. For example, as Mishkin et al. state: "if both habits and memories are constantly being formed by experience in normal animals, then the great debate between behaviorists and cognitivists will have finally been resolved in favor of both parties" (p. 73). That is, we (like many simpler life forms) not only employ our VCS and CSS to adapt, but we also simultaneously tap our CLS and acquire knowledge in a cognitive fashion. So learning is quite a variety of things. These include all the ways in which experience is capturable by the plasticity of the brain (see Levin and Vuckovich, 1987), as well the changes (on a large scale, or system level) of organization of the brain. And we aspire eventually to be able to correlate psychological development with such changes within the brain (see Levin, 1987). A further reason for paying attention to the system source of learning is that, if we are to ever fully understand our patients and their learning blocks we must learn to recognize the "fingerprints" of the major learning subsystems of the brain involved.

III

Research by Galin (1974), and Broughton (1975) supports the correlation noted in the preceding section between REM sleep, dreaming, and activation of the right cerebral hemisphere. Bakan (1978) seems to have been the first to suggest that during REM sleep periods the right hemisphere is released from left-hemisphere control, a point I have used in my own speculations regarding the effects of this release on "review" and "downloading" activities of important learning subsystems (see the previous section). Flor-Henry (1983) presents data supporting the corollary view to Bakan's position, namely, that during development the left hemi-

sphere asserts control (dominance) over the right hemisphere during waking activity and that this is part of what
prevents the acting out of forbidden sexual and aggressive
impulses. Of course, during sleep the potential for acting out
is substantially reduced.

Bertini (1982) shows that subjects differ widely in their
use of sleep and waking states in information processing.
Specifically, he notes that whereas there are some persons
"for whom dream mentation is strictly associated to REM
[periods]," there are others "for whom this association is
much less strict or rigid." (p. 59) Bertini, using a unilateral
tactile recognition task, concludes that *there is in general "a
right hemisphere dominance during the REM state"* (p. 59, italics
added). He further notes that "people who exhibit strong
lateralization during wakefulness are also the people who
show strong REM specialization" (p. 59).

This kind of correlation, supported by Galin's (1974) and
Broughton's (1975) work, is appealing, because it fits with
what is already known about the right hemisphere's special
capacities for gestalt formation, spatial perception, and man-
agement of affect (through its preferential connection with
the limbic system). However, before one can conclude that
REM dreaming is led by a system primarily determined by
the right hemisphere, one needs to review allegedly contra-
dictory evidence. In this regard, Antrobus, Erlichman,
Wiener, and Wohlman (1982), using EEG monitoring, assert
that "visual imagery is [actually] stronger as the left, not the
right, hemisphere becomes dominant!" (p. 51). Accordingly
they "do not find support for the general arousal or state
dependent models with respect to . . . EEG activation [of the
right hemisphere]" (p. 51). In addition, Lavie and Tzischinsky (1986), investigating the relationship between cognitive laterality and REM sleep, conclude that "dreaming
cannot be seen as a right hemisphere function" (p. 353). Of
course, the claim being made is not that all dreaming is right

hemispheric, but rather that REM dream states seem to be a reflection of the right hemisphere's activity, at least in certain individuals. Reading the fine print, however, one is less convinced about the arguments of Lavie and Tzischinsky. For one, they did confirm that as far as right-handers (but not left-handers) are concerned that subjects awakened during REM periods did better on tests of right-hemisphere function (p. 355). Moreover, left-hemisphere kinds of testing also discriminated when right-handed subjects were awakened during NREM periods (pp. 355–357). Rather than disproving the hypothesis being questioned, these findings seem to qualify it, much as Crow's (1986) work on schizophrenic twin studies in England has shown that there is concordance between temporal lobe abnormalities and right-handed identical twins, but not left-handed identical twins. It seems to me that a reasonable conclusion is that REM dreams and right hemisphere activation are probably closely correlated, at least in right-handed people. This should not be taken to mean, however, that dreaming is a right-hemisphere phenomenon; but rather that the right hemisphere seems to be a leading edge in the REM type of dreaming, so that its "release" is an important element in the information processing and exchange between (learning) subsystems of the brain. It is my feeling that understanding the organization of such subsystems ought to be our highest priority. This was the goal when Vuckovich and I (1983) reviewed interhemispheric communication from a psychoanalytic perspective; and this is the critical part of our paper (Levin and Vuckovich, 1987) on brain plasticity and learning, where we consider the possible role of the cerebellum and its nuclei in bridging the hemispheres and thus coordinating some of the brain's learning activity.

Finally, an article by Ehrlichman, Antrobus, and Weiner (1985) needs to be mentioned to complete the review of the research critical of the right hemisphere activation/REM dream hypothesis. One problem in this research is that the authors use an EEG power asymmetry measurement technique developed for studying waking subjects and then apply it to identification of hemispheric activation in sleeping subjects, a task whose certainty they themselves recognize as difficult (p. 482). A second problem lies in their extraordinary idea that "dreams are not primarily visual phenomena" (p. 483), an assumption that seems questionable in the extreme. On top of this, they then contradict themselves by suggesting that "the visual aspect of dreams cannot be denied" (p. 483), changing their minds primarily because they now wish to argue that REM sleep dreams cannot possibly be right hemispheric because some data suggest to them that the visual imagery system involves in part some left-hemispheric functions. Finally, they make the unlikely inference that "mentation in REM [sleep] is continuous with that in waking [life] and will thus show the same patterns of hemispheric involvement as would comparable cognitive activities in waking" (p. 483). This latter assertion, I believe, is contradicted by a large mass of sleep and dream research that establishes beyond doubt that what is happening during sleep and dreaming states is quite different in its organization and impact from waking mentation, such that disturbing these sleep/dream (e.g. REM) states clearly has an impact on learning acquisition. In short, Ehrlichman and his colleagues fail to be convincing, and even if they are correct in some particulars their work seems off the main line.

At this point, I wish to move from dreams and communication within and between brain subsystems to the subject of (REM) dreams and learning per se. W. C. Stern (1970) shows with early REM deprivation studies that there is a clear correlation in humans between REM deprivation (RD) and learning impairment. This subject is also reviewed by Smith (1985), who covers animal research, which finds the same clear correlation between RD and learning impairment.

Stern's work further quotes studies by Dewan and by Gardner to the effect that one can conclude without much doubt that *"new memories are [primarily] processed and encoded during REM sleep"* (p. 255), that is, during our REM dreams. Dushenko and Sterman (1984) present further experimental support for Bakan's theory that *REM sleep deprivation works against learning primarily by its impact on the right hemisphere, which is in "cyclic ascendence" during REM sleep* (p. 25). *That is, REM and NREM cycles represent cyclic alterations in the connectedness and communications between the two cerebral hemispheres, and by inference, between the leading information processing/learning subsystems of the brain noted earlier in this essay.* (For additional discussion of some of these issues, which are beyond the scope of this brief essay, the reader is referred to Klein and Armitrage, 1979, Levin and Vuckovich, 1987, and Levin, 1987).

To round out this discussion of sleep and dream research, let us consider some basics regarding the circadian sleep wake cycle and its regulation. Gross (1982) reviews this subject in depth, noting that the basic pacemaker in man is set for 25 hours and is probably controlled by an oscillator in the hypothalamus (p. 21), itself a subsystem of the brain of extraordinary complexity. Entrainment phenomena are mediated visually by a retinohypothalamic projection to the suprachiasmic nuclei (SCN) (p. 21). A number of substances, including vasoactive intestinal polypeptide found in high concentrations in SCN cells, probably play a key role in inducing sleep (p. 26). Borbely (1986) discusses research on endogenous sleep substances. He basically conceptualizes sleep, however, as a product of a sleep-dependent process (process S) and a circadian oscillator (process C). How these processes are connected pharmacologically, and how they relate to dreaming, is not specifiable, except as reviewed in the first parts of this essay. Jouvet (1982) pursues 5 hydroxytryptophan (and other indolamines), which plays a critical but as yet incompletely understood role, along with peptides and other "hypnogenic factors" (p. 93) in controlling sleep rhythms. Sakai (1984) adds that two different populations of cells in the medial part of the nucleus reticularis magnocellularis "are closely tied to transitions into and out of paradoxical [i.e. REM] sleep" (p. 4). Put another way, Sakai is telling us that pontogeniculoccipital (PGO) waves "located in the caudal mesencephalic and rostral tegmental structures" (p. 5) of the pons are associated with vivid dreaming in man and other mammals. Most important for psychoanalysis, and contrary to the views of Hobson and McCarley (1977), the localization of this PGO system does not explain dreaming, nor does it in any way invalidate psychoanalytic insights into dreams, which have been obtained by a unique methodology, namely, clinical psychoanalytic experience. What this research does clarify is that the postural atonia occurring during REM periods is secondary to the "tonic excitation of supraspinal inhibitory systems" (p. 10) associated with PGO activity. And the ascending reticular system originally described by Moruzzi and Magoun (1949) "also plays an important role in the mechanism underlying cortical desynchronization during PS [paradoxical sleep, which is the same as REM sleep]" (Sakai, p. 14).

A third complication is that hypothalamic, hypophysial control should not be ignored in trying to understand these phenomena of sleep and dreams. Makara, Palkovits, and Szentagothai (1980) report on "hypothalamic endocrine angio architechtonics" (pp. 306–311), a field that describes the computerlike, modular structure of parts of the hypothalamus and hypophysis, which mediate between external and internal milieus by means of both humoral and neural circuitry. A very large number of hormones and neuroactive substances, including a number that are affected during "shock" or stress are controlled by this system of neurohypophysis and hypothalamus (Makara et al., 1980). There is no question, then, that if we are eventually to better understand the relationship between sleep and dreams—and include in this an understanding of the relationship between stress, nightmares, and information processing (as written about so cogently by Max Stern)—we need to fathom this particular neurology as well, so that along with our precious psychoanalytic perspectives we can eventually truly understand how fear bothers sleep. But at the very least we know that the brain is composed of multiple learning systems that become alternately connected and disconnected from each other for purposes that appear to relate to REM (dream) periods of "reviewing" and NREM periods of "downloading" critical insights. Eventually, if our anxiety can be quelled, we then "recreate symbolically from a knowledge base novel reconstructions of our world" (Foulkes, 1983, p. 405) with obvious adaptive value. If our analysis of our situation tells us that our brain is headed toward a dangerous situation and we need some help, then we experience nightmares; and if our development has included "bio-trauma," such that we expect no help will be forthcoming, then we may pass over into pavor nocturnus. Often critical in individual cases is whether the human environment will allow one to tap one's maximum potential for emotional growth.

We have now returned full circle to Stern and his theorizing about *Repetition and Trauma*. I agree with his final conclusion, that whereas for the individual there is no requirement of traumatic frustration for development to occur, for the species "the inevitable experience of trauma was absolutely necessary to the development of an innate program capable of generating anticipation." That is, over the course of human evolution trauma has led to physiological defenses against shock. The purpose of these defenses is to provide, first, a signal mechanism "in the form of agitated behavior (such as one has during a nightmare or pavor nocturnus attack) . . . and . . . primary depression . . ." and second, "external assistance in the face of disorganizing states of tension." This is the teleonomic principle that Stern has unraveled, and it is an example of the kind of creative interdisciplinary theorizing that I personally believe is not only valuable in individual clinical psychoanalytic work, but central as well to the continuing health and growth of psychoanalysis itself.

REFERENCES

Altman, L. L. (1975), *The Dream and Psychoanalysis,* rev. New York: International Universities Press.

Antrobus, J., Ehrlichman, H., Wiener, M. & Wollman, M. (1982), The REM report and the EEG: Cognitive processes associated with cerebral hemispheres. In: *Sleep 1982,* ed. W. P. Koella. Basel: Karger, pp. 49–51.

Arkin, A. M. (1978), Editor's commentary on chapter 16. In: *The Mind in Sleep: Psychology and Psychopharmacology,* ed. A. M. Arkin, J. Antrobus & S. J. Ellman. Hillsdale, NJ: Lawrence Erlbaum Associates, pp. 542–546.

Aserinsky, E. & Kleitman, N. (1953), Regularly occuring periods of eye motility and concommitant phenomena during sleep. *Science,* 118:273–74.

Bakan, P. (1978), Dreaming, REM sleep and the right hemisphere: A theoretical integration. *J. Altered States of Consciousness,* 3:285–307.

Basch, M. F. (1983), The perception of reality and the disavowal of meaning. *Annual of Psychoanalysis,* 51:125–153. New York: International Universities Press.

Berger, L. (1967), Function of dreams. *J. Abn. Psychol.,* Monograph 5:1–28.

Berger, R. J. (1970), REM sleep and mechanisms of oculomotor control. In: *Sleep and Dreaming,* ed. E. Hartmann. Boston: Little, Brown, pp. 277–294.

Bertini, M. (1982), Individual differences in the information-processing modes in sleep and waking states. In: *Sleep 1982,* ed.W. P. Koella. Basel: Karger, pp. 57–62.

Borberly, A. A. (1986), Endogenous sleep substances and sleep regulation. *J. Neural Transmission,* (sup.) 21:243–54.

Broughton, R. J. (1975), Biorhythmic variations in consciousness and psychological functions. *Canadian Psych. Rev.,* 16:217–239.

Crow, T. J. (1984), Left brain, retrotransposons, and schizophrenia. *Brit. Med. J.,* 293:3–4.

Desmedt, J. E. (1979), *Progress in Clinical Neurophysiology. Vol. 6: Cognitive Components in Cerebral Event-Related Potentials and Selective Attention.* Basel: Karger.

Dewan, E. M. (1970), The programming hypothesis for REM sleep. In: *Sleep and Dreaming,* ed. E. Hartmann. Boston: Little, Brown, pp. 295–307.

Dushenko, T. W. & Sterman, M. B. (1984), Hemisphere-specific deficits on cognitive/perceptual tasks following REM sleep deprivation. *Internat. J. Neurosci.,* 25:25–45.

Ehrlichman, H., Antrobus, J. S. & Weiner, M. S. (1985), EEG asymmetry and sleep mentation during REM and NREM. *Brain and Cognition,* 4:477–485.

Emde, R. (1983), The pre-representational self and its affective core. *The Psychoanalytic Study of the Child,* 38:165–192. New Haven: Yale University Press.

Fisher, C., Byrne, J., Edwards,A. & Kahn, E. (1970), A psychophysiological study of nightmares. *J. Amer. Psychoanal. Assn.,* 18:747–782.

Flor-Henry, P. (1983), *Cerebral Basis of Psychopathology.* Littleton, MA: Wright-PSG.

Foulkes, D. (1983), General discussion: Dream psychology. In: *Sleep Disorders: Basic and Clinical Research,* ed. M. Chase & E. D. Weitzman. New York: Spectrum, pp. 401–413.

Freud, S. (1900), *The Interpretation of Dreams. Standard Edition,* 4 & 5. London: Hogarth Press, 1953.

_____ (1916/1917), *Introductory Lectures in Psychoanalysis. Standard Edition,* 15 & 16. London: Hogarth Press, 1963.

_____ (1920), *Beyond the Pleasure Principle. Standard Edition,* 18:7–64. London: Hogarth Press, 1955.

Friberg, L. & Roland, P. E. (1987), Functional activation and inhibition of regional cerebral blood flow and metabolism. In: *Basic Mechanisms of Headache,* ed. J. Olesen & L. Edvinsson. Amsterdam: Elsevier.

Frick, R. B. (1982), The ego and the vestibulocerebellar system: Some theoretical perspectives. *Psychoanal. Quart.,* 60:93–122.

French, T. M. (1952), *The Integration of Behavior*, Vol. 1. Chicago: University of Chicago Press.

Friedman, S. & Fisher, C. (1967), On the presence of a rhythmic, diurnal, oral instinctual drive in man: A preliminary report. *J. Amer. Psychoanal. Assn.*, 15:317–343.

Fromm, E. (1947), *Man for Himself*. New York: Rinehart.

Gabel, S. (1985), Sleep research and clinically reported dreams. Can they be integrated? *J. Anal. Psychol.*, 30:185–205.

Galin, D. (1974), Implications for psychiatry of left and right cerebral specialization. *Arch. Gen. Psychiat.*, 31:572–583.

Gastaut, H. & Broughton, R. (1965), A clinical and polygraphic study of epidosic phenomena during sleep. In: *Recent Advances in Biological Psychiatry*, Vol. 7, ed. J. Wortis. New York: Plenum, pp. 197–220.

Greenberg, R. (1970), Dreaming and memory. In: *Sleep and Dreaming*, ed. E. Hartmann. Boston: Little, Brown, pp. 258–267.

Gross, G. (1982), Regulation of the circadian sleep-wake cycle. In: *Sleep 1982*, ed. W. P. Koella. Basel: Karger, pp. 19–29.

Henderson, J. L. & Wheelwright, J. B. (1974), Analytic psychology. In: *American Handbook of Psychiatry*, vol. I, ed. S. Arieti. New York: Basic Books, pp. 809–819.

Hillyard, S. A. (1979), Event-related brain potentials and selective information processing in man. In: *Progress in Clinical Neurophysiology, Vol. 6: Cognitive Components in Cerebral Event-Related Potentials and Selective Attention*, ed. J. E. Desmedt. Basel: Karger, pp. 1–52.

Hobson, J. A. & McCarley, R. W. (1977), The brain as a dream state generator: An activation-synthesis hypothesis of the dream process. *J. Amer. J. Psychiat.*, 134:1335–1348.

Jouvet, M. (1982), Hyponogenic indolamine-dependent factors and paradoxical sleep rebound. In: *Sleep 1982*, ed. W. P. Koella. Basel: Karger, pp. 21–28.

_____ (1984), Indolamines and sleep-inducing factors. In: *Sleep Mechanisms: Experimental Brain Research*, Supp. 8, ed. A. A. Borbely & J.-L. Valatx. Berlin: Springer, pp. 81–94.

Kahn, E., Fisher, C. & Edwards, A. (1978), Night terrors and anxiety dreams. In: *The Mind in Sleep: Psychology and Psychopharmacology*, ed. A. M. Arkin, J. Antrobus & S. J. Ellman. Hillsdale, NJ: Lawrence Erlbaum Associates, pp. 533–542.

Klein, R. & Armitage, R. (1979), Rhythms in human performance: 1 and 1/2 hour oscillations in cognitive style. *Science*, 204:1326–1328.

Kohut, H. (1971), *The Analysis of the Self.* New York: International Universities Press.

Lassen, N. (1987), Cerebral blood flow measured by xenon-133. *Nucl. Med. Comm.*, 8:535–548.

Lavie, P. & Tzischinsky, O. (1986), Cognitive asymmetry and dreaming: Lack of relationship. *Amer. J. Psychol.*, 98:353–361.

Levin, F. M. (1987), Psychological development and the [changing] organization of the brain. Paper presented to the Chicago Psychoanalytic Society, May 26.

_____ & Vuckovich, M. (1983), Psychoanalysis and the two cerebral hemispheres. *The Annual of Psychoanalysis*, 11:171–197. New York: International Universities Press.

_____ & _____ (1987), Brain plasticity, learning and psychoanalysis. *The Annual of Psychoanalysis*, 15:19–96. New York: International Universities Press.

Makara, G. B., Palkovits, M. & Szentagothai, J. (1980), The endocrine hypothalamus and the hormonal response to stress. In: *Selye's Guide to Stress Research*, Vol. 1, ed. H. Selye. New York: Van Nostrand Reinhold, pp. 280–337.

McClintock, B. (1984), The significance of response of the genome to challenge. *Science*, 226:792–800.

Meissner, W. (1966), Hippocampal functions in learning. *J. Psychiat. Res.*, 4:235.

Mishkin, M., Malamut, R. & Bachevalier, J. (1984), Memories and habits: Two neural systems. In: *Neurobiology of Learning and Memory*, ed. G. Lynch, J. L. McGough & M. Weinberger. New York: Guilford, pp. 65–77.

Moruzzi, G. & Magoun, H. W. (1949), Brain stem reticular formation and actuation of the EEG. *Electroencephalogr. Clin. Neurophysiol.*, 1:455–473.

Rechtschaffen, A. (1983), General discussion: Dream psychophysiology. In: *Sleep Disorders: Basic and Clinical Research*, ed. M. Chase & E. D. Weitzman. New York: Spectrum, pp. 401–413.

Roland, P. E. & Friberg, L. (1985), Localization of cortical areas activated by thinking. *J. Neurophysiol.*, 53:1219–1243.

Rothstein, A. (ed.) (1986), *Reconstruction of Trauma: Its Signficance in Clinical Work.* New York: International University Press.

Sakai, K. (1984), Central mechanisms of paradoxical sleep. In: *Sleep Mechanisms: Experimental Brain Research*, Supp. 8, ed. A. Borbely & J.-L. Valatx. Berlin: Springer, pp. 3–18.

Slap, J. W. & Trunnell, E. E. (1987), Reflections on the self state dream. *Psychoanal. Quart.*, 56:251–262.

Smith, R. C. (1985), Sleep states and learning: A review of the animal literature. _Neurosci. Biobehav. Rev._, 9:157–168.

Squire, L. R. (1986), Mechanisms of memory. _Science_, 232:1612–1619.

———— Cohen, N. J. & Nadel, L. (1982), The medial temporal region and memory consolidation: A new hypothesis. In: _Memory Consolidation_, ed. H. Weingartner & E. Parker. Hillsdale, NJ: Lawrence Erlbaum Associates, pp. 185–210.

Stern, W. C. (1970), The relationship between REM sleep and learning: animal studies. In: _Sleep and Dreaming_, ed. E. Hartmann. Boston: Little, Brown, pp. 249–257.

Szentagothai, J. (1975), The module concept in cerebral archetecture. _Brain Research_, 95:475–486.

Tobler, I. (1984), Evolution of the sleep process: A phylogenetic approach. In: _Sleep Mechanisms: Experimental Brain Research, Supp. 8_, ed. A. A. Borbely & J.-L. Valatx. Berlin: Springer, pp. 207–226.

Tolpin, M. (1983), Toward the metapsychology of injured self-cohesion. Presented to meeting of Chicago Psychoanalytic Society, Feb. 22.

———— & Kohut, H. (1980), The disorders of the self: their psychopathology of the first years of life. In: _The Courses of Life: Psychoanalytic Contributions Towards Understanding Personality Development and Early Childhood_, ed. S. I. Greenspan & G. H. Pollock. Washington, DC: National Institute of Mental Health.

Tolpin, P. (1983), Self psychology and the interpretation of dreams. In: _The Future of Psychoanalysis: Essays in Honor of Heinz Kohut_, ed. A. Goldberg. New York: International Universities Press.

Trevarthen, C. (1979), The tasks of consciousness: How could the brain do them? _Mind and Brain_, CIBA Foundation Series 69, Excerpta Medica.

———— (1985), Facial expressions of emotion in mother-infant interaction. _Human Neurobiol._, 4:21–32.

Wasserman, M. D. (1984), Psychoanalytic dream theory and recent neurobiological findings about REM sleep. _J. Amer. Psychoanal. Assn._, 32:831–846.

Winson, J. (1985), _Brain and Psyche: The Biology of the Unconscious_. Garden City, NY: Anchor Press/Doubleday.

1

Pavor Nocturnus

T he pavor nocturnus of children and the night terror of adults, each of which can be defined broadly as an awakening in fright from a severe nightmare, represent expressions of anxiety of an intensity rarely witnessed directly in daytime intercourse, still less often in the analytic consulting room. Until the development of laboratory dream research in the mid-1950s, when for the first time the student of dreams had direct access to the sleeper and accordingly an opportunity to investigate his physiological experience at first hand and his psychological experience as reported immediately upon awakening, psychoanalytic commentators on night terror and pavor nocturnus had to rely largely on anecdotal reports from diverse sources and the impressionistic accounts of their own patients. The latter accounts, apparently in keeping with the traumatic nature of the nocturnal episode and the amount of time intervening between the occurrence and its report, generally provided but meager descriptions of the content of the nightmare preceding the attack. Even when the elicited content was more substantial, it was of a type rather different from that of the wish-fulfilling dreams that are the staple of the psychoanalytic interpretive method. Content was straightforward, if invariably sensational, and showed little of the elaborate and bizarre visual imagery and fantastic wordplay of the wish-fulfilling dream, in apparent support of Freud's (1920) claim that traumatic nightmares were an exception to the wish-fulfilling nature of dreams. These accounts further suggested relatively little remembrance on the part of the patient of the attack itself—a retrograde amnesia, as it were, for events witnessed at first hand by parents, siblings, and spouses, and including, in the severest cases, bloodcurdling screams and somnambulism. Psychoanalysis, then, so largely concerned with the problem of neurosis, was practically impotent to examine one of the most striking expressions of the affect *par excellence* of neurosis, anxiety.

Although laboratory dream research has done much to remedy this situation, it is not without its own limitations of method—to which I shall refer later—having to do principally with the artificiality of the laboratory setting itself. Perhaps because of this, reports of such research tend generally to give short shrift to the subjective experience of the sleeper; anxiety is rated and quantified rather than described. Inasmuch as it is the anxiety that has attracted our interest in the first place, we are put as readers in the awkward position of having to judge a phenomenon whose terror has been abstracted and relativized. It might be best, then, to begin by presenting a composite portrait of the subjective experience of night terror—pre-1960, as it were—which we shall very often have to qualify, drawn as it is from the impressionistic accounts I mentioned earlier. Nevertheless, I think it will prove a useful device for orienting the reader to this most perplexing of human behaviors.

It seemed certain, before 1960, that night terror attacks were always preceded by a dream. In general, the stronger and more threatening the predominant sensations of the subsequent attack, the weaker was the recollection of the dream. The dream usually contained elements having reference to motility—running, climbing, gliding, falling, and the like. We often encountered scoptophilic and exhibitionistic fantasies and oral elements that were subsequently specifically represented in the anxiety accompanying the ensuing attack: fears of being eaten, of being unable to scream, of being choked. Auditory elements—speaking or being spoken to, hearing noises—were also noted.

As the dream unfolded it suddenly revealed its nightmarish character, in the form of a threat against the sleeper: attacks by humans, animals, ghosts, vampires; walls closing in on him, waves engulfing him, his crashing down from heights or being crushed by unknown powerful forces. Invariably the sleeper was helpless against the threat, which was nearly always connected with the most severe anxiety.

This feeling of helplessness was then experienced as having the character of reality, although still remaining in some way hallucinatorily connected with the ongoing nightmare. The sleeper attempted to scream, to cry for help, but was unable to utter a sound. He sought to fight back, but in vain. He was paralyzed, unable to breathe, with a sensation of dreadful pressure on the chest, similar to the precordial fear of annihilation; he had a sensation as though a band of iron were encircling his head, and a conviction of being overwhelmed by unconsciousness. Now he was certain that he was no longer dreaming, that he really was in the utmost peril. He knew that he would be able to save himself from this peril by waking up, but he could not wake up and with each passing moment felt the real end coming closer. He gathered himself for a last attempt at escape but could not move his body or limbs – until suddenly, with some violent effort, he woke to reality. Covered with perspiration, his heart racing madly, his breast heaving, he felt he had escaped a mortal danger.

The reader familiar with the literature may have noticed the more than passing resemblance between this composite description of night terror and Ernest Jones's (1931) definition of nightmare as a distressing dream necessarily showing, among other features, three cardinal ones: agonizing dread, a sense of oppression and weight upon the chest that alarmingly interferes with respiration, and a conviction of helpless paralysis. Freud (1895) also noted difficulty in breathing and sweating as features of the adult night terror and elsewhere (1900) described a case of pavor nocturnus in a 13-year-old boy whose sleep was interrupted by severe attacks of anxiety accompanied by hallucinations: "He would wake up from an anxiety dream in terror, unable to cry out at first, until his voice came back to him and he was distinctly heard to say 'No, no, not me!' " (p. 586). More recent psychoanalytic investigators have noted that the most severe night terror attacks are often accompanied by sleepwalking (Stern, 1951; Sperling, 1958; Mack, 1965; Schur, 1969).

The foregoing composite portrait invites the obvious question: Are the sensations of helpless paralysis, difficult breathing, and pressure on the chest based on actual physiological events? In imprecise but convenient shorthand, are they real? Real or not, do they instigate the *observed* responses of ample breathing, pounding heart, and violent movement? And, finally, given these questions, how can we delimit the attack itself? When does it begin and the nightmare end? We shall see that the results of laboratory dream research suggest answers to these questions. For the time being, however, I should like to propose that the pavor nocturnus attack, even while remaining hallucinatorily connected to the content of the nightmare, includes the features noted by Jones—agonizing dread, a sensation of difficult breathing, real or not, and a conviction of helpless paralysis, real or not—to which must be added the accelerated heart rate, ample respiration, and scream or violent movement that appear to end the attack, with somnambulism reserved for the severest cases. The definition recommends itself if only for being comprehensive.

I should now like to consider the questions I have raised in the light of a condition in which psychic events lead to a temporary breakdown in vital somatic functions. I refer to what has been variously called "primary shock" or "neurogenic shock of central origin." In this condition, overintense mental activity leads to a series of physiological events that resemble the sensations or physiological events described in the pavor nocturnus attack. The discussion is based on the seminal research on stress conducted by Selye and his co-workers (1946, 1947, 1950) in the aftermath of World War II.

SHOCK AND COUNTERSHOCK

Selye (1950) defines "systemic stress" as a condition in which "due to function or damage—extensive regions of the body deviate from normal resting state" (p. 9). He postulates that any stress mobilizes two responses: a specific one that seeks to alter the threat by producing an alloplastic change—a change in the environment—and a nonspecific systemic autoplastic response, called the "alarm reaction" and defined as the sum of all nonspecific phenomena elicited by sudden exposure to stimuli to which the organism is quantitatively or qualitatively not adapted. The alarm reaction is thus independent of the nature of the damaging agent and represents a response to damage as such. When stress is sufficient to overwhelm the defensive capabilities of the alarmed organism, it eventuates in full-blown shock: There is profound weakness, flaccidity of muscles, pallor, perspiration, a weak rapid pulse, and a low arterial blood pressure. As the reaction progresses, this deficiency affects the nervous system as well as other parts of the organism, paralyzing its functions: reflexes are abolished, there is no response to painful stimuli, the subject is lethargic or semicomatose, the respiration becomes shallow and weak, and the blood pressure declines to zero. As the condition progresses further, there is stupor or coma, and finally death (Moon, 1942, p. 24). Most authors conceive of full-blown shock in terms of anoxia and circulatory failure and *"a condition of depression of the vital activities of the body, associated with a marked and progressive fall in blood pressure"* (Rose and Carless, quoted by Moon, 1942, p. 43). Although primary shock arising from psychic activity is much less severe than secondary shock—blood volume does not so precipitously decline and the primary circulatory disturbance of lowered blood pressure is usually only of short duration—it can lead to secondary shock with fatal consequences; Moon reports that death from circulatory failure occurs in various forms of psychopathology in which demonstrable lesions are lacking (p. 214). It should be noted that the "clinical features, functional disturbances, and visceral changes are almost identical whether death has occurred rapidly by shock or more gradually after grave illness: . . . Shock is merely the approach of death by its usual mechanism" (p. 214).

Selye (1949, 1950) subdivides the alarm reaction into two more or less distinct phases: *shock,* an initial manifestation of systemic damage, and *countershock,* a defensive homeostatic response to the damage. The phase of shock is characterized by lowered body temperature and lowered blood pressure, depression of the nervous system, decrease in muscle tone, deranged capillary and cell membrane permeability, decreased blood volume due to a loss of fluids to the tissues, and gastrointestinal disturbances. The vasomotor center in the medulla sends out efferent vasoconstrictor and vasodilator impulses to the blood vessels by way of the spinal cord and sympathetic nerves, causing a fall in blood pressure followed by a disturbance of fluid balance through increased capillary and cell membrane permeability. When blood pressure and blood volume thus decline, physiological reactions take place that tend to compensate for the deficiency. These make up the phase of countershock.

Selye found that adrenocorticotropic hormone (ACTH) plays a major role in the defense of the body against systemic injury. Stimulation of the hypothalamus, which regulates vital autonomic activities, produces (1) intensified activity in the sympathoadrenal system and (2) strong reactions in the skeletal effectors of the body. (1) Increased secretion of adrenaline results in the release of corticotropic hormone from the anterior lobe of the pituitary gland. In response to corticotropin, the adrenal cortex enlarges, and secretion of cortical hormone is augmented. Organic corticoids produce changes in organic and inorganic metabolism; inorganic corticoids cause retention of sodium with resultant increase in blood volume, a plethora that contributes to elevation of blood pressure. (2) Stimulation of the caudal portion of the hypothalamus causes increased muscular activity. When experimentally induced in animals, hypothalamic stimulation resulted in a reaction termed "sham rage" consisting of struggling, biting, spitting, snarling, clawing movements, lashing of the tail, dilation of the pupils, increased blood sugar, rapid heart rate, rise in blood pressure, and increased secretion of adrenaline. Wortis and Mowrer (1942) reported cases of human sham rage as a result of uninhibited hypothalamic discharge. Inasmuch as the defensive role of adrenaline consists in increasing circulatory activity and oxygen supply, it may be said to facilitate muscular activity; increased muscular activity in turn intensifies the secretion of adrenaline and its effect on the adrenal cortex.

The successful defense of the organism against stress thus shows an exquisite balancing of homeostatic forces. Even the initial phase of shock seems to serve a signal function. In reviewing it, one is inevitably reminded of Freud's (1926) description of signal anxiety, wherein the ego submits "to a slight attack of the illness in order to escape its full strength" (p. 162). In general, Selye seems to have been deeply influenced by Freud's ideas on trauma as I characterize them in Chapter 3.

Selye (1950) also noted, however, that there is an antagonistic effect of various corticoids. Desoxycorticosterone (DCA), for example, at first increases the excitability of the nervous system; in a second phase, it produces a reversible depression. "If very large doses of DCA suddenly enter the blood stream . . . there is a preliminary stage of excitation followed by [an] *anesthesia* [so deep] that major operations can be performed . . . [under it]. In certain experimental conditions, DCA produced a state of *experimental catalepsy*" in rats. DCA-treated rats, for example, showed extraordinary hypersensitivity and irritability with profuse salivation. They jumped or bit when the experimenter attempted to hold them. "After this they fell to the floor apparently in an unconscious state" (pp. 666–668).

All of this, I submit, is remarkably like the sequence of events we observe in infants subjected to severe deprivation. In the early infantile period, frustrations such as loss of mothering or delayed sucking are responded to by three different forms of primitive stress reaction, which follow one another according to the degree of frustration experienced: (1) *agitation,* consisting of mass activity, restlessness, startle pattern, crying, vigorous body movements, and muscular tension; (2) *catatonoid reaction,* consisting of refusal to suck, breathing difficulties, constipation, hypertension, and rigidity of all body muscles with an extensor reaction of the muscles of the back, interspersed with periods of violence and screaming, culminating in; (3) *full shock*, with stupor, general loss of muscle tone and of reflex excitability throughout the body, pallor, gastrointestinal disturbances (diarrhea), and death (Ribble, 1939, 1941). We see, that is, the identical sequence of excitation and depression observed in DCA-treated rats and in humans in full-blown shock; and we see it not only in the general movement from agitation to full shock, but also in the intervening catatonoid stage, wherein violent activity is interspersed with inhibition. The catatonoid reaction thus seems to recapitulate in microcosm the general trend in the development of full-blown shock. One might even describe the entire sequence as "catato-noid."

The catatonoid reaction is so named because of its resemblance to the more well-known catatonic syndrome, first described by Kahlbaum. In this, stupor, immobility and rigidity, and vegetative disorders—of the circulatory, respi-ratory, and digestive systems—are interspersed with occa-sional brusque impulsions (raptus). There is decreased me-tabolism and temperature, lowered blood pressure, bradycardia, difficulty breathing, loss of appetite, refusal of food, constipation, increased muscle tone but lowered mus-cular and cerebral activity, and the characteristic states of extreme motor excitement alternating with depersonalized stupor.

It is highly significant, I think, that all the substances that were used experimentally to produce catatonia (adren-aline, acetylcholine colibacilli, and so on) have likewise been found effective for the experimental induction of shock (de Jong, 1945; Baruk, 1949). Could it be that catatonia repre-sents the last phase in a long line of defenses against shock? The catatonoid reaction itself seems to result from a blocking of higher cortical centers, probably as a consequence of anoxia, and represents a biological regression to a more vegetative existence, a dedifferentiation of the organism. Some of its manifestations are reminiscent of the rigidity observed in decerebrate animals (Sherrington, 1906), and it corresponds to the reaction of "dead faint" in animals, a kind of catatonic stupor known as "fright rigidity." Its defensive function can be understood in terms such as these: Anoxic decortization diminishes in some degree the action of the cortex and thus the registration of inflowing stressful stimuli. Since the organism as a whole functions as a sensorimotor unit, this blocking causes a paralysis of controlled—of volitional—motor activity. At the same time, however, the increased tone of the muscular system, resulting from stimulation of lower brain centers, causes an increase in the supply of adrenaline. Catatonic rigidity thus facilitates respiration and steps up the supply of oxygen, which in turn facilitates the uncontrolled impulsions characteristic of the disorder. There is, in other words, a minimum of energy output, as reflected in lowered metabolism, with a very high order of muscular capacity and the same exquisite balance of homeostatic forces we saw in Selye's countershock, but at a much lower, more primitive level.

Let me summarize our findings so far: The alarm reaction consists of sequential phases of inhibition and excitation—there is the depression of function of the initial phase of shock, followed by the agitation of the countershock phase. The first is a physiological alert mechanism, the second a restitutive response to alarm. If we hypothesize a similar alert mechanism in the frustrated infant, then the reaction of agitation can be seen to serve the countershock function. The succeeding catatonoid reaction would then represent yet another phase of inhibition—at least with regard to the characteristic stupor, vegetative disorders, and rigid immobility—and yet another phase of excitation—the paroxysmic motor impulsions. The sequence, then, would be inhibition (initial phase of shock), excitation (agitation response), inhibition (catatonoid depression of function), and excitation (catatonoid impulsion). Hereinafter I shall refer to the complex of agitation and catatonoid reaction as countershock.

I must now anticipate my argument to some extent by stating that laboratory dream research has unequivocally established that the pavor nocturnus attack proper takes place in a "modified waking state" in which the "subject is dissociated, is relatively unresponsive to the environment, shows decreased cortical responsiveness, and may be delusional and/or hallucinating" (Fisher, Kahn, Edwards, and Davis, 1974a, p. 388)—in a condition of stupor, in other words. The relevance of this to the foregoing should be apparent. If we define the catatonoid reaction, in its essence, as a condition of stupor and increased muscle tone with paroxysmic motor impulsions, have we not defined a condition very much like the complex of *observed* responses in pavor nocturnus? In particular, the violent movement and, as we have now seen, dissociated, stuporous state observed in the full-blown attack? Do we not find in both conditions the same curious coexistence of motility and stupor? There are, moreover, certain casual descriptive correspondences between the two conditions: the sensations of helpless paralysis—possibly rigid—difficult breathing, and pressure on the chest of pavor nocturnus, with the rigid immobility, difficult breathing, and vegetative disorders of the catatonoid reaction. The accelerated heart and respiratory rates observed in pavor nocturnus would be consistent with a preceding agitation phase. Might it not be the case, then, that the helpless paralysis reported by victims of pavor nocturnus is in fact the rigid immobility of the catatonoid reaction, a form of catalepsy? Might this not be an actual physiological event—however fleeting, howevermuch hallucinatorily connected to the preceding nightmare—one that, if it does not quite "instigate" the observed responses of rapid breathing, pounding heart, and violent movement, is connected in some causal way to those responses? For note what is to my mind a crucial point: The alternating phenomena of the catatonoid reaction—the rigid immobility and brusque impulsions both—are *defensive* reactions consistent with our understanding of countershock in general, its alternating phases of agitation and inhibition, although at a primitive developmental level. What I am suggesting, in sum, is that pavor nocturnus as I have defined it, is a countershock reaction and, as such, a nocturnal defense against shock.

Now the reader may object that I have failed to consider an important question: Is there any evidence of an *initial* shock phase, serving a signal function, in the pavor nocturnus complex? To answer that question I shall have to refer to the laboratory dream research that I have put off reporting till now. Accordingly, the next section is devoted to a consideration of that research.

LABORATORY DREAM RESEARCH

In the mid-1950s it was demonstrated that in a high percentage of instances dream reports were elicited when laboratory subjects were aroused from sleep associated with rapid conjugate eye movements, or REM sleep. During these periods, which recur about every 90 minutes in the sleep cycle and occupy 20 to 25 percent of the total sleep of young adults, there is intense cellular activity in the cortex and other parts of the nervous system, with a 30 to 50 percent higher blood flow through the brain than in non-REM periods. Heart and respiratory rates increase and become highly variable, and there is a marked loss of muscle tone and a virtually complete absence of motility, with some evidence that motor pathways to the periphery are blocked as a result of descending inhibitory impulses originating in the brain stem (Mack, 1970). The electroencephalogram of REM sleep produces low-voltage desynchronized recordings, in contrast to the large, so-called slow, or delta, waves of Stages III and IV. The latter stages, occurring in the first few hours of sleep, constitute the deepest phases of non-REM sleep and make up 25 percent of total sleep. Heart and respiratory rates are basal (Roffwarg, Musio, and Dement, 1966), and muscle tone is only partially reduced (Fisher et al., 1974b) in Stages III and IV.

In 1965 Gastaut, R. and Broughton, R. J. demonstrated that somnambulism, enuresis, and the pavor nocturnus of children and adults occur during extremely intense spontaneous arousals from Stage IV sleep, arousal defined as a condition in which brain waves are of a waking alpha pattern. They typically recorded a burst of delta-wave activity, followed by ample alpha rhythms, several ocular movements, blinking, very high heart and respiratory rates, and movement followed by intense global muscular contraction. Total cessation of breathing for up to five seconds was sometimes observed. A guttural cry and further body movement subsequently marked the return of respiration and the subsidence of motor and autonomic components. The subject invariably showed decreased cortical responsiveness to visual stimulation, an incapacity to integrate sensory input, and the following other characteristic symptoms: (1) mental confusion and disorientation; (2) automatic behavior; (3) poor response to efforts to provoke behavioral wakefulness; (4) retrograde amnesia for many intercurrent events, screams or sleepwalking among them; and (5) fragmentary recall of apparent dreams or none at all (Gastaut and Broughton, R. J., 1965). These findings, which have been replicated for the most part, but not entirely, in other laboratories, were significant for showing that sleepwalking, enuresis, and pavor nocturnus were not associated with dreaming, at least "if dreaming is defined as the mental activity of the REM periods. . . ." (Fisher, Byrne, Edwards, and Kahn, 1970, p. 750).

The question then became whether mental activity of any kind gave rise to these events, particularly in light of their sudden onset and the fifth symptom mentioned above, fragmentary or no recall of apparent dreams. Broughton (1968) reported that subjects of pavor nocturnus attacks tended to have a relative tachycardia during slow-wave sleep and hyperactive heart rate after arousal, which suggested to him the possibility that the mental content elicited after an attack may have been elaborated in response to those or other, related physiological events. In other words, the subject may have produced mental content of being attacked or crushed in response to the physiological event of a pounding heart or difficult breathing. Broughton argued that such attacks may thus arise out of a "psychological void": Anxiety may be a "secondary response to certain physiological events such as polypnea, apnea, and palpitation rather than the reverse—a somatic terror reaction that occurs in response to, or in conjunction with, a terrifying idea," to use Mack's (1970, p. 190) formulation. A key piece of evidence for this claim was the finding that mental content, when it was recalled, consisted generally of a single, unelaborate scene.

It is difficult to exaggerate the dismay at this conclusion of psychoanalytically oriented students of pavor nocturnus. It may even have approached Freud's reaction to the discoveries that caused him to abandon the seduction hypothesis. Broughton's proposal obviously plays havoc with my own view that pavor nocturnus represents a defense against stress caused by threatening nightmares. We need not, however, take so drastic an action as Freud's: Research conducted in Fisher's laboratory in the late 1960s and early 1970s disconfirmed several of the key findings on which

Broughton's proposal was based. Before turning to that research, let me urge the reader to bear in mind throughout the ensuing discussion that Gastaut and Broughton were first to the question and, accordingly, set the terms of the debate. Fisher et al. (1970, 1974a, b; for convenience sake, Fisher hereinafter) acknowledge explicitly that their own efforts were directed toward confirming or disconfirming Gastaut and Broughton's findings.

Fisher (1974a) confirmed the finding that pavor nocturnus arises out of Stage IV sleep: The *"Stage 3–4 arousal-reaction night terror . . .* includes the night terrors of children and adults and a minority of the night terrors of posttraumatic neurosis" (p. 387). (When Fisher refers to "Stage 3-4" he means to indicate that night terrors were observed in spontaneous arousals from both stages of sleep. In general, however, night terror attacks, or what I call pavor nocturnus, are associated with Stage IV sleep [Fisher, 1970, 1974a]. The pavor nocturnus of posttraumatic neurosis is considered in Chapter 3.) He also generally confirmed Gastaut and Broughton's (1965) findings as to the physiological events associated with the attack:

> Following a gasp, with a break in the respiratory rhythm, and the onset of screaming and change to verbalization, the subject passes into an *arousal reaction* associated with alpha waking EEG. . . . There is intense autonomic discharge, heart rate doubling or nearly tripling, up to 160 or 170/min. Such levels may be attained within 15 to 30 seconds, and may constitute the most rapid acceleration of heart rate known to man. The episodes are shortlived, heart rate decelerating within 45 seconds to 1½ mins. and returning to normal baseline levels within two to four minutes. There is a tremendous increase in respiratory amplitude and a moderate rate change [Fisher, 1974a, p. 388].

In the laboratory, moreover, "onset of Stage 4 night terrors is almost always associated with massive body movement" (p. 331). The postarousal symptoms observed by Gastaut and Broughton were also generally confirmed by Fisher:

> The subject is dissociated, relatively unresponsive to the environment, shows decreased cortical responsiveness, and may be delusional and/or hallucinating. . . . There are varying degrees of amnesia for content of the night terror and the behavioral manifestations associated with it [p. 388].

It is, of course, the last symptom that most concerns us: How great is the degree of amnesia for content of the night terror? Fisher (1974b) reported that he was able to obtain a mean of 58 percent recall of mental content for Stage IV pavor nocturnus arousals, demonstrating that recall was much better than Broughton (1968) had claimed. His finding was consistent with other studies showing good recall of apparent sleep mentation after nonspontaneous Stage III–IV arousals. Fisher was also concerned about showing, however, that such content was not necessarily elaborated in response to postarousal physiological events, but was rather evidence of ongoing mentation *preceding* the attack. That this was so was suggested by numerous examples of a close resemblance between recalled mental content and the sleep utterances recorded during the episode, as in the case of a night terror "in which the vocalization aspect indicated that someone was stepping on (the subject), subsequently reported as the content of the night terror" (p. 185). This finding too was supported by other studies demonstrating a high degree of concordance between sleep speech and recalled mental content after nonspontaneous Stage III–IV arousals, implying that the sleep utterances were a manifestation of prior ongoing sleep mentation. Screams, curses, and cries for help appropriate to concordant sleep utterances were also noted, lending further support to the idea of ongoing prior mentation, although Fisher was careful to add that there were many instances in which recalled content was not concordant and others in which the content apparently was elaborated during the postarousal period in response to autonomic discharge (p. 174). In a few instances, "nontraumatic" mental content was recalled that appeared to have developed just prior to the onset of the episode, and in other instances "the subject reported that the frightening content caused him to scream and initiated the episode" (p. 174).

All of this argued for the positive side of the equation, the idea that sleep mentation preceded the attack. As for the negative side of the equation—that content was not elaborated in response to postarousal physiological events—Fisher noted that while

> the content of night terror frequently consists of a single scene or thought, there were many reports of traumatic content unique and unusual, quite elaborate and dreamlike, sometimes consisting of one or more scenes in sequence, and very unlikely to have originated in the postarousal period in response to physiological sensation or environmental conditions [p. 174].

This too generally was in accord with studies showing that mental content elicited from non-REM sleep was different from that of REM sleep in being "less lengthy, elaborate, bizarre, implausible, visual and emotional, but more thoughtlike and conceptual in nature and concerned with recent events of the preceding day"; all the same, "in some 10 percent of NREM awakenings, content may be dreamlike, difficult to differentiate from that of REM periods" (p. 176).

In a previous study, moreover, Fisher (1970) had demonstrated that recalled content of night terrors was "coherent,
psychodynamically organized, related to the subject's preex-
isting traumata and conflicts, and to the REM dreams of the
same night" (p. 779). This would argue against a prearousal
"psychological void," and by implication, against postarousal secondary elaboration. To that same point, Fisher
reported that he had been unable to replicate Broughton's
(1968) finding that Stage IV night terror subjects showed "a
relative tachycardia during slow-wave sleep" (p. 779;
Broughton [1970] subsequently reversed himself on this
score). In fact, subjects tended to exhibit a slight *decrease* in
autonomic activity before the attack, with slower and less
variable respiration preceding the more severe night terrors,
and heart rates as low as 44–48/min. in some subjects (Fisher,
1974a, p. 390). Finally, Fisher (1974b) was able to argue
persuasively that the lack of a gradual buildup of the night
terror—its abrupt onset—"does not militate against the possible role of ongoing Stage 4 mentation in triggering it. Such
mentation may touch upon an intense conflict area, producing a terrifying image or thought, *suddenly* igniting intense panic" (p. 174).

Fisher (1974a) concluded that the

> full-blown Stage 4 night terror is a fight-flight episode
> combining sleep-talking, sleep-walking, and halluci-
> nated and delusional mental content associated with
> terror. . . . It is ushered in by loud piercing screams of
> bloodcurdling and animallike intensity, associated
> with verbalizations, cries for help, cursing, moans,
> groans, sighs, etc. . . . [and a] sudden, cataclysmic
> breakthrough of uncontrolled anxiety [p. 388].

He suggested that the night terror was *"not a dream at all in
the ordinary sense, but a symptom, a pathological formation of*

NREM sleep, which is describable as a rift in the ego's capacity to control anxiety . . . [and] seems to be a manifestation of the failure of mastery" (p. 395).

Clearly, Fisher's findings as to content were sufficient to discredit the idea that pavor nocturnus arises out of a psychological void, entirely in response to autonomic activation. The major objection to my formulation has thus been removed. I should now like to compare that formulation with Broughton's and Fisher's findings taken together, insofar as they do not conflict, in a test of its compatibility with contemporary research.

In this composite laboratory picture, the sequence of events is evidently this: (1) a gasp, with a break in the respiratory rhythm (Fisher); (2) alpha waking EEG, with stupor (Fisher and Broughton); (3) ocular movements and blinking (Broughton); (4) scream or other vocalization (Fisher); (5) intense autonomic activation (Fisher and Broughton); (6) body movement followed by intense global muscular contraction (Broughton); (7) apnea up to five seconds (Broughton); (8) guttural cry and return of respiration (Broughton); (9) massive body movement (Fisher and Broughton); (10) subsidence of motor and autonomic components (Fisher and Broughton). It ought to be acknowledged immediately that the list is misleading in two respects, due entirely to its composite nature. The notation for Fisher at (9) owes to the fact that he does not observe events (6), (7), or (8); his finding of massive body movement would properly occupy the slot immediately after intense autonomic activation in a sequence based exclusively on his research. For the same reason, Broughton's "guttural cry" (8) is probably identical to Fisher's "other vocalization" (4). Gastaut and Broughton (1965) conceive of sleeptalking as a form of pathology more or less distinct from pavor nocturnus and do not regard vocalization as a response to terrifying dream mentation, the combination of which probably accounts for their lesser emphasis on vocalization in their descriptive reports. Finally, all these events happen very rapidly, so that the very idea of there being a sequence is to some extent misleading. Nevertheless, some such sequence can always be identified, and I doubt that either Fisher or Broughton would object to the list I have proposed, so long as the appropriate qualifications are made. I might add that both authors obviously agree on the question of anxiety in relation to pavor nocturnus, which is described as intense whether it arises in response to sleep mentation or autonomic activation.

Let me now break down the list in terms of my countershock complex of agitation response and catatonoid reaction.

Agitation Response.   The gasp and break in the respiratory rhythm, indicating the onset of intense autonomic activation, the alpha waking EEG, the ocular movements and blinking, the scream or other vocalization, and the body movement preceding the contraction are all manifestations of excited activity. Each can be viewed as serving a defensive function in response to stress resulting from a preceding nightmare. The gasp and accelerated heart and respiratory rates are consistent with a response to depressed circulatory activity; the eye and body movements testify to the restoration of muscle tone (recall that muscle tone is partially reduced during Stage IV sleep [Fisher, 1974b]) and therefore of the motility defense against shock. The only possible exception I can see to the characterization of these events as constituting an agitation response is the condition of stupor associated with the waking state. Why should stupor be evinced in a condition of increased autonomic activation? But perhaps we are putting the question the wrong way. Would it not be better to say that stupor is a *manifestation* of the circulatory depression to which autonomic activation responds? In this sense, decreased cortical responsiveness and incapacity to integrate sensory input would be manifestations of cortical anoxia.

Catatonoid Reaction. In event (6) of the list we can observe the transition from the agitation response to the catatonoid reaction: The body movement is followed by an intense global muscular contraction; agitation is succeeded by inhibition. This is of course the identical sequence of events observed in catatonia proper, so it might be more accurate to speak of event (6) as the first manifestation of the catatonoid reaction as a whole. It hardly matters in any case, however, inasmuch as given the alternating responses of the catatonoid reaction as I have defined it, it will inevitably—by definition—appear to overlap with the preceding agitation phase.

Now, the reader will surely have remarked that Fisher's name does not appear next to any of the entries (6) through (8). Although he does not state explicitly that his findings disconfirm Broughton's on these matters of global muscular contraction, apnea, and return of respiration, neither does he provide any evidence in support of them. He does state, in his paper on mental content (1974b), that "of the three classical symptoms of nightmare mentioned by Jones . . . (a) intense dread, (b) paralysis, and (c) oppression on the chest, only the first has been found characteristic of the night terror" (p. 187; also 1970, p. 754).

All three of Broughton's findings are of course paramount to my thesis, inasmuch as they accord with my view that sensations of rigid paralysis and difficulty breathing are characteristic features of both pavor nocturnus and the catatonoid reaction in the countershock defense. I have already suggested that the sensation of helpless paralysis experienced by subjects of pavor nocturnus attacks is in fact the rigid immobility of the catatonoid reaction, a form of

catalepsy. The intense global muscular contraction reported
by Broughton would confirm that view. So too would a total
cessation of breathing confirm it indirectly, as well as directly
confirming difficult respiration and a sense of oppression on
the chest. All these features are consonant, moreover, with
the defensive function of catatonoid inhibition that I have
already described.

Fisher (1974b) documented many examples of choking
content, which he acknowledged could be viewed as responsive to respiratory difficulty (p. 181). He also discussed a
subject who in half his arousals "reported strong physiological sensations and difficulty breathing" (pp. 181–185). In
both these cases, however, Fisher probably referred to
respiratory difficulty associated with increased amplitude
and rate of respiration, since those were the only forms of
respiratory change his measurements recorded. Presumably
he was able to determine that the subject who reported
difficulty breathing was referring specifically to increased
amplitude and rate of respiration, and not to an interference
with breathing, as I would have it.

In that same paper, moreover, Fisher stated that many
of his night terror subjects had reported mental content of
being crushed (p. 186) or entrapped (p. 179). Although he
did not regard such contents as responsive to postarousal
physiological events—as he did in the case of choking—could
we not apply to the former the same logic of concordance he
used for the latter? That is to say, could we not view mental
content of being crushed or entrapped as responsive to a
postarousal physiological event of intense global muscular
contraction with apnea? It is true that choking is a more
direct rendering of difficult respiration (but of ample respiration?) than being crushed or entrapped would be of rigid
paralysis. But can there *be* a more direct rendering of that
experience short of the subject's saying he felt paralyzed? A
list of some of the contents Fisher reported will give the

reader a flavor for the issues at stake: Subject 1's contents included "being hit by a train, engulfed by books, squeezed between a wall and a bus, and walls or unnamed objects closing in . . . 'I was in a tomb' " (p. 181); Subject 2's contents included "being stepped on by the experimenter . . . the room shrinking and coming down on him, or someone being trapped in a small box" (p. 181); Subject 3's contents included "that he was dying" (p. 181; associated by Fisher to postarousal palpitations); Subject 6 reported that "the hull of a ship came down and he was caught beneath it, in darkness, not crushed, but enclosed and trapped" (p. 182); Subject 7's "most severe arousal was about a window closing in and the room getting smaller and smaller" (p. 182); Subject 12's "most fearful arousal . . . was that a shelf in the room was closing in" (p. 182). All these contents, I submit, can be interpreted in terms of a postarousal secondary response to sensations of rigid paralysis—all the more so in a situation such as this where "measurements" of paralysis "events" are inherently ambiguous and subjective, much more so, at any rate, than the measurements of heart and respiratory rates that Fisher did take. In this regard, I ought to point out that Fisher's postarousal interviews of his subjects began with the question "What was just going through your mind?" (1974b, p. 177), not "What were you just feeling?" The former question, it seems to me, would invite an answer framed in terms of mentation rather than sensation and would, for that reason, discourage a direct report of a feeling of immobility.

Part of the problem here may be that Fisher's subjects apparently reported very little indeed in the way of content, at least as compared to patients in psychoanalysis (a matter I shall discuss in more detail in Chapter 2). Since he was concerned with rebutting the notion that autonomic factors gave rise to the attack, as Broughton claimed, what content he had was forced to serve as evidence of prearousal mentation, when it might just as well have served as evidence of postarousal secondary elaboration. Note, finally, that in making this argument I am only exploiting the very standard of concordance that Fisher used to make his case for prearousal mentation. Although his standard may appear to be more exacting than mine—he required a "repetition of or a reference to verbal content that appeared in the sleep utterances" (pp. 182–183)—it may again be the case that a more direct rendering of the experience of paralysis was not available to the subject, as I suggested earlier.

Nevertheless, Fisher explicitly rejects Jones's claims for helpless paralysis and oppression on the chest and, by implication, Broughton's findings as to muscular contraction, apnea, and return of respiration. In fact, both of Jones's symptoms

> are more prevalent in the REM nightmare. Rather than feelings of paralysis, the night terror is frequently characterized by the presence of motility and somnambulism. The marked loss of muscle tone during REM sleep is probably responsible for feelings of paralysis during REM nightmares [1974b, p. 187].

In support of this latter assertion Fisher adduces no evidence of REM-nightmare content referring to paralysis in any of the three articles under consideration. If such evidence did exist, moreover, it would contradict the very substantial evidence that anxiety in REM nightmares does not arise in response to physiological conditions—evidence, I might add, that Fisher exploits from the reverse perspective to support his conception of a desomatization mechanism in REM sleep (1974a, p. 371). Needless to say, then, in the face of their all-too-apparent disagreement on this score and the questions I have raised above, I prefer Broughton's findings to Fisher's, at least until future research decides the matter definitively.

It remains for me now to describe the succeeding phase of catatonoid excitation in the pavor nocturnus shock defense. This can be found in event (9), the massive body movements reported by both Fisher and Broughton, which correspond to the catatonoid brusque impulsions that invariably follow the condition of rigid immobility. In the pavor nocturnus complex, in other words, the sleeper typically sits bolt upright in his bed. This may or may not be followed by somnambulism and is, in either case, consonant with the previously discussed defensive function of catatonoid excitation. The attack comes to an end with the subsidence of motor and autonomic components (10). Note that my formulation is able to provide a causal explanation for the coexistence of motility and stupor, in the defensive functioning of movement in the countershock reaction.

The reader will recall that in my closing remarks in the last section I implied that laboratory dream research would produce evidence of an initial manifestation of shock in the pavor nocturnus complex, serving a physiological signal function. In this regard I would note the highly suggestive finding reported by Fisher that night terror subjects tend to exhibit a slight decrease in autonomic activity before the more severe attacks, with slower and less variable respiration and lower heart rates, of which he observes "it is as if the episode arises out of a physiological vacuum, there being no gradual buildup" (1970, p. 755; "physiological quiescence" in 1974a, p. 331). Although Fisher states that the correlation of lower heart and respiratory rates during this prearousal period is positive but not statistically significant, he goes on to report evidence that REM-nightmare subjects show a moderate tachycardia during Stage IV sleep (p. 391). That is to say, subjects with more severe pavor nocturnus attacks show heart rates before the attack not only lower than normal but also lower than the *higher-than-normal* rates of subjects not afflicted with such attacks. This difference was statistically significant (p. 357). Fisher also notes that respiratory rates of REM-nightmare subjects during Stage IV sleep are also higher than normal and that the difference on this measure between them and night terror subjects is also positive, although not statistically significant (p. 359). I believe this evidence, taken together, strongly suggests a prearousal autonomic deficit in pavor nocturnus subjects consistent with the idea that stress associated with threatening dream content results in an initial manifestation of shock. We have seen that this initial manifestation is always expressed in autonomic inhibition, can occur in response to psychic events, and leads to an anoxia that can be shown to be the cause of stupor such as that found in pavor nocturnus. Fisher's discussion of the same data is addressed in Chapter 2.

This concludes my argument in favor of the counter-shock defense formulation. I have demonstrated its compatibility with contemporary laboratory research and its usefulness as an explanatory model for pavor nocturnus. It ought to be noted at once that the picture of pavor nocturnus thus presented is very different from what our patients' reports have led us to expect. First, vocalization apparently occurs at the onset of the attack, in contrast to the occasional impression and common-sense presumption that screams denote the end of the attack. Our patients' lack of recall for vocalization at the earlier point should not surprise us, however, inasmuch as Fisher emphasizes that "there is almost always a complete amnesia for the talking, screaming, cursing and other sleep utterances ushering in the night terror" (1974b, p. 186). Second, far from instigating the observed reactions of rapid breathing and pounding heart, the sensations of rigid paralysis, difficulty breathing, and pressure on the chest arise in *response* to those events, in terms of the causal model of defense I have outlined. Third, anxiety is not associated at first with *accelerated* heart and respiratory rates, as we have always assumed, but rather with lowered rates on both measures. Surely our commonsense presumptions on both these scores could not have been overturned without the benefit of laboratory dream research.

2

Regression Explanations

In *Beyond the Pleasure Principle,* Freud (1920) concluded that repetitive posttraumatic dreams did not serve the function of fulfilling wishes but were

> helping to carry out another task, which must be accomplished before the dominance of the pleasure principle can even begin. These dreams are endeavouring to master the [traumatic] stimulus retrospectively, by developing the anxiety whose omission was the cause of the traumatic neurosis [p. 32].

In Chapter 3 I shall consider Freud's analysis in *Beyond the Pleasure Principle* in some detail, with reference to the frequently observed repetitive character of pavor nocturnus and night terror attacks. Here, by way of orienting the reader to the theoretical issues raised by the laboratory results reported earlier, I want to discuss the alternative explanation of such attacks offered by Fisher in 1970.

Fisher begins his 1970 study—which demonstrates the repetitive nature of the Stage IV night terror—by noting that Freud's investigation of posttraumatic dreams had "rather fateful consequences for him leading to his major theoretical formulations about the repetition compulsion and the death instinct" (p. 747). He concludes the same study by observing that

> the Stage IV nightmare does not serve to master anxiety, but rather represents a massive failure of the ego to control it. We agree with Freud that the posttraumatic nightmare is some sort of exception to the wish-fulfilling theory of dreams, but do not believe that it operates beyond the pleasure principle, under the domination of the repetition compulsion, nor that it supports the theory of the death instinct. We suggest that the Stage IV nightmare *is not a dream at all in the ordinary sense,* but a relatively rare symptom, a pathological formation of NREM sleep [p. 781].

In a later (1974a) paper he states:

> We have stressed the remarkable quiescence of autonomic activity during the Stage IV sleep which just precedes the eruption of the night terror. This eruption is *describable* as contingent on regression of various ego functions, and there may be a connection, which at present defies precise definition, between the autonomic slowing and the regression [p. 379].

Fisher's formulation, then, is in terms of *symptom formation* and *regression*: "The Stage IV nightmare is . . . a pathological formation . . . ," sleep brought about by a rift in the ego's capacity to control anxiety" (1970, p. 777).

Now I think we can agree that there is a regression of ego functioning in the "modified waking state" that follows arousal from the Stage IV nightmare: After arousal, in other words, the "subject is dissociated, relatively unresponsive to the environment, shows decreased cortical responsiveness, and may be delusional and/or hallucinating" (Fisher, 1974a, p. 388). In 1970 Fisher also described the affective and behavioral aspects of postarousal ego regressions:

> In M. Schur's (1958) terms, there is regression from potential or present danger to the traumatic situation with feelings of helplessness, uncontrolled anxiety and panic, and full resomatization of the anxiety response. Desperate attempts to escape from the traumatic situation are observed with cries for help, the subject regressing even to calling for mother, and to primitive flight reactions in the form of being propelled out of bed and running [p. 767].

With the exception of the remark concerning regression "from potential or present danger to the traumatic situation," and the related characterization of the anxiety response as "resomatized," these are all manifestations of postarousal ego regression repeatedly observed in the laboratory and outside it. Whether one regards "regression to the traumatic situation" as having taken place, on the other hand, depends on one's inferences from those observations.

Fisher next asks, "What triggers these severe nightmares that arise instantaneously in a violent cataclysmic fashion?" (p. 767) and answers as follows:

> It is suggested that the condition for their onset is increasing ego regression brought about by the pro-

gressive deepening of Stage IV sleep. From the psychological side, sleep results in regression of various ego functions: weakening of defense, especially repression, loss of reality testing, appearance of primary process, etc. Ego regression is fostered as Stage IV deepens in the early hours of the night when fatigue is greatest. There is a remarkable correlation between the severity of the nightmare and certain physiological conditions, e.g., the more severe the nightmare the longer the period of Stage IV preceding it, the larger the amount of delta waves and the slower the respiration [and heart] rate (1970). Thus, although it appears that the Stage IV nightmare grows out of a physiological vacuum, this is misleading. It is true that no cardiac or respiratory activation that might be associated with anxiety is taking place, but rather the opposite, physiological changes indicative of deeper sleep, and therefore capable of bringing about regressive changes in the ego. Under these conditions there occurs in predisposed individuals a massive eruption of repressed anxiety connected with previous traumatic experiences of either the shock or strain variety, of recent origin, or regressively reactivated traumatic fixations of very early childhood [p. 767].

Prearousal ego regression, then, is the "condition" for the Stage IV night terror.

Let us first consider whether there have been any *observations* of prearousal ego regression in Stage IV sleep, such as have been made of ego regression after arousal. We have already seen, for instance, that after arousal, the Stage IV night terror subject is relatively unresponsive to his environment. What of the prearousal relationship between the subject and his environment? Fisher (1970) reports: "The arousal threshold during Stage IV sleep in severe nightmare subjects is considerably lower than during REM sleep, whereas normally the opposite is the case" (p. 768). This finding was based on the results of an experiment in which a buzzer was sounded during the REM and Stage IV sleep of night terror subjects. Whereas the non-night terror subjects of Zimmerman's (1970) study were more responsive to arousal-provoking external stimuli during REM sleep than NREM sleep, the subjects of Fisher's experiment were more responsive to such stimuli during NREM sleep. That is to say, night terror subjects demonstrated a greater than usual responsiveness to their environment during such sleep, which hardly argues for prearousal ego regression if one of the measures of such regression is responsiveness to the environment. Note that this is no less direct an observation of the state of the ego than is the observation of postarousal unresponsiveness; it requires no inference on our part as to that state.

Now compare this observation with Fisher's evidence for ego regression before arousal, which consists of inferences from observations of physiological conditions, on the presumption that "from the psychological side, sleep results in regression of various ego functions." Thus there are "physiological changes indicative of deeper sleep, and therefore capable of bringing about regressive changes in the ego." On the level of observation, it is clear that we can say nothing more than that certain changes have been noted in the functioning of the cardiorespiratory and nervous systems. On the level of inference, we must ask, first, whether the observed physiological changes are indeed indicative of the subject's "deeper" sleep, when the same subject has been shown to be more easily aroused from such sleep by external stimuli. Fisher (1974a) acknowledges this problem:

> The lower arousal threshold during delta sleep in these subjects further confuses the issue of the

"depth" of sleep, and stands in seeming contradiction to other observations, such as the finding of longer stretches of Stage 4 preceding night terrors, which we have interpreted as possibly indicating "deeper" sleep [p. 382].

In the same study, moreover, he notes that the two most severe night terrors ever recorded occurred in the virtual absence of Stage IV sleep as measured by delta wave amplitude (p. 374).

Second, even if we grant the inference of deeper sleep, we must ask whether observation supports the further inference that deeper sleep is "capable of bringing about regressive changes in the ego." Given the presumption that "sleep results in regression of various ego functions" and the inference of deeper sleep preceding night terror attacks, we should expect to observe greater ego regression during the Stage IV sleep of night terror subjects than during the REM sleep of subjects with anxiety or ordinary wish-fulfilling dreams. In this regard, let us consider the three examples of ego regression Fisher suggests.

(1) Appearance of Primary Process.

Fisher (1970) states: "In addition to the recovery of dream reports from some 80 to 90 percent of arousals made from REM periods, mental activity, generally less dreamlike and more secondary process in nature, has been shown to go on during nondreaming sleep" (p. 749). Later he (1974b) states:

> Mental content of NREM sleep differs from that of REM sleep in being less lengthy, elaborate, bizarre, implausible, visual and emotional, but more thought-like and conceptual in nature and concerned with recent events of the preceding day. However, in some

10 percent of NREM awakenings, content may be dreamlike, difficult to differentiate from that of REM periods [p. 176].

Mack (1970) remarks that "of the terrifying episodes that awaken us in the night, those that are richer in hallucinatory dream *content* seem more likely to occur during REM sleep" (p. 192). Mack adds:

Various authors have found that non-REM awaken-ings tend to yield reports that are less bizarre, less affective, more like ordinary thought—or secondary process thinking in psychoanalytic terminology—and more concerned with the contemporary lives of the subjects. Rechtshaffen et al. have shown that non-REM mentation often may resemble ordinary back-ground thinking. If, as has been repeatedly sug-gested, dreams reflect an effort to resolve conflict and to integrate present experiences with earlier memories and conflicts, the availability of active primary process mechanisms during REM periods could be useful toward this end. Conversely, in non-REM sleep peri-ods, directly disturbing daytime experiences or day residues that have revived early traumatic events could not be as extensively modified or transformed by the regressive, symbolic mechanisms of dreaming [pp. 192–193].

All these quotations, of course, indicate that NREM sleep, far from giving evidence of the appearance of primary process, show the opposite, a kind of thought that "often may resemble ordinary background thinking." REM periods, in contrast, demonstrate "the availability of active primary process mechanisms," the "regressive, symbolic mecha-nisms of dreaming"; the mentation of such periods is "richer

in hallucinatory dream content" and more "elaborate, bizarre, implausible, visual and emotional." It is true that most
of these observations were made of NREM sleep in general;
they were not observations of the prearousal mental content
of night terror subjects. All the same, let us consider them in
relation to the posited connection between depth of sleep
and ego regression. If it is true, as Fisher (1970, p. 767) states,
that "ego regression is fostered as Stage IV deepens in the
early hours of the night when fatigue is greatest," then why
do awakenings from such "deeper" sleep yield reports
offering little or no evidence of primary process thought, that
is to say, of regression? Conversely, why do dream reports
from REM periods, when sleep is supposedly "shallower,"
show precisely such thought and, consequently, regression?
Even if it is the case, moreover, that "in some 10 per cent of
NREM awakenings, content may be dreamlike, difficult to
differentiate from that of REM periods," this would only
demonstrate that regression during the former periods occurs more or less to the same extent that it does in the latter
periods; it would not demonstrate greater regression in
"deeper" NREM sleep.

Now let us consider the prearousal mentation of Stage
IV night terror subjects and REM anxiety dream subjects as
revealed by their dreams. Do the nightmares of the former
show more primary-process thinking than the nightmares of
the latter? Fisher (1970) reports:

> Primary process mechanisms are utilized in both. The
> traumatic events that produce nightmares rarely ap-
> pear in undisguised form either in the REM or NREM
> nightmare. Subject E represented the rape by a series
> of uncontrolled natural phenomena, such as storms
> and volcanic eruptions. The choking scene which
> precipitated S's nightmare never occurred in it but
> was replaced by a threatening man standing at the

foot of the bed holding a knife, the latter undoubtedly
having symbolic sexual meaning. Symbolizations, displacements, and condensations appear in both the
REM and NREM nightmares [p. 774].

Obviously there is nothing in this indicating a greater degree
of primary-process thinking in NREM and REM nightmares.
On the face of it, indeed, it appears that the greater degree of
primary process thought occurred in the REM anxiety
dreams of Subject E, which "dealt repetitively with the rape
in distorted and disguised ways," (p. 765). The rape was
variously represented by a train that invaded the room, by
uncontrolled natural phenomena, a storm or flow of fiery
lava, or by some curtains that choked her, a displacement
from the rapist to the curtains that separated the room from
the terrace. In contrast, Subject S's Stage IV nightmares
developed following an experience of being choked into
unconsciousness by her violent, jealous, paranoid boyfriend.
The repetitive content of her nightmare was of a man
standing at the foot of the bed (where in reality the choking
episode occurred) often with a knife in his hand (p. 765).
Thus, although the choking scene that precipitated S's
nightmare never occurred, surely that scene was represented
in a much less "disguised" and "distorted" way in her
dreams than the original rape was represented in E's. Even
the "reality elements" of these nightmares—the "curtains"
and "foot of the bed," respectively—reveal this difference:
The foot of the bed did not, as it were, attack Subject S in her
dreams. I should add that these observations of prearousal
mental content were no less direct than observations of
postarousal "delirium and/or hallucination."

In fact, it is difficult to see the basis for Fisher's claim that
"symbolizations, displacements, and condensations appear
in both the REM and NREM nightmares." The repetitive
night terrors of Subject R in the 1970 study—of choking on an

electrode or on something "cut or severed"—which Fisher interprets in terms of oral aggression, can certainly be more plausibly explained in light of the fact that the subject had, five years before, undergone "an operation for thyroid cancer and bears a huge, rather ugly scar on his neck" (p. 763). It is hard to see how this event could have been represented in less undisguised fashion, with less primary process distortion, unless we are willing to admit Fisher's rather fanciful interpretation that the electrode represented a "symbolic displacement from the body or body parts of the experimenter" (p. 762). We seem to have in this dream an explicit demonstration of Mack's suggestion that "in non-REM sleep periods, directly disturbing daytime experiences or day residues that have revived early traumatic events [cannot] be as extensively modified or transformed by the regressive, symbolic mechanisms of dreaming" (1970, p. 193).

(2) Weakening of Defense, Especially Repression.

In the context of the foregoing discussion Fisher (1970) remarks: "In general, naked manifestations of drive, especially aggression, are more marked in the NREM nightmare than in the REM anxiety dream" (p. 774), "naked" implying, to my mind, that such manifestations of "drive" have not been "extensively modified or transformed by the regressive, symbolic mechanisms of dreaming." The same observation, however, can also support an inference of ego regression in the sense of "weakening of defense, especially repression," as can each of the observations of lesser primary process thinking I have discussed. In other words, the lesser "disguise" and "distortion" of Subject S's NREM nightmares suggest a relative failure of repression as compared to the REM nightmares of Subject E. This is because the dream work has always been viewed as a "compromise formation of unconscious wishes and preconscious day residue, distorted by the influence of censorship" (Schur, 1966, p. 167); it is the "process which, with the co-operation of the censorship, converts the latent thoughts into the manifest content of the dream (Freud, 1925, p. 45).

On this point, then, I agree with Fisher: Any explanation of night terror attacks must be couched in terms of failure of repression. But the nature of that failure is very much open to question, whether, for example, it involves a "weakening" of defense of greater magnitude than occurs in sleep generally, or whether it should be laid to the nature of the "latent thought" itself. The distinction is crucial: I dispute the necessity of attributing a lack of repression to ego regression, as implied by Fisher's conception of "weakening." It should rather be attributed to inadequate development, as I demonstrate in Chapter 3. There too I shall show that the relationship between the "latent thought" and inadequate development underlies Freud's entire discussion of the repetition compulsion in *Beyond the Pleasure Principle* and can serve as the basis for a more coherent explanation of the observations that have been made of pavor nocturnus than Fisher's conception of ego regression. To give but one example: On Fisher's account, regression must lead both to the appearance of primary process thinking and a weakening of repression, when a weakening of repression would be expected to result in a *lesser* appearance of primary process. At the same time, his explanation contradicts the clinical and experimental evidence for just such a lesser appearance of primary process distortion in night terror attacks. Let me stress that I do not dispute the evidence for regression after arousal or that inadequate development is invariably the basis for regression in the classical sense. My argument is with Fisher's use of the construct in the much narrower sense of prearousal ego regression as a consequence of "deeper" sleep. This usage relies on an assumption of psychophysiological parallelism that has no observational foundation.

It also leads to a model of dream anxiety that exhibits at least one striking anomaly. I can demonstrate this with reference to Fisher's (1974a) observation that anxiety-dream subjects show higher than normal heart and respiratory rates during undisturbed REM sleep (pp. 354, 357, 359; see also p. 326 on method). Put another way, normal subjects with ordinary wish-fulfilling dreams show less autonomic activity during undisturbed REM sleep than do anxiety-dream subjects. Now, if higher cardiorespiratory rates are associated with "shallower" sleep and depth of sleep is associated with regression, we would expect to observe that the REM anxiety dream subject is less regressed than his normal counterpart; that is to say, "defense, especially repression" should be stronger in him than in the subject with ordinary wish-fulfilling dreams. Of course, the very opposite is the case: The outbreak of anxiety in the former subject is, according to Fisher's logic, a demonstration of a failure of repression. The subject whose heart and respiratory rates are supposed to indicate *less* regression is observed to be more regressed. It is no answer to this to point to the ostensibly different content of wish-fulfilling dreams. This is because the very conception of such dreams requires that the contents associated with the wish must previously have been repressed; in turn, repression implies that such contents must at one time have represented danger. Accordingly, all wish-fulfilling dreams are potentially anxiety provoking. The only credible answer to this observation would have to rely on the presumption that higher cardiorespiratory rates in REM anxiety-dream subjects represent ongoing but muted, or free-floating, anxiety. But then the very basis for Fisher's inference of regression in Stage IV night terror subjects would fall away: The higher rates of REM anxiety-dream subjects would no longer be evidence of "shallower" sleep, capable of limiting regression, but of "anxious/regressed" sleep. The comparability of the two types of sleep would thus be thrown into question and, with it, the inference of regression. So too would the evidence of higher rates in such subjects contradict the presumption from which the inference derives, that "on the psychological side, sleep results in regression of various ego functions": These rates are higher than normal *waking* rates.

I think we can begin to see from the foregoing one of the cardinal demerits of approaches based on the assumption of psychophysiological parallelism: One could plausibly maintain that REM anxiety dreams have their source in the higher heart and respiratory rates to which certain individuals are prone during sleep. On such a theory, all such dreams would be symptoms, no more nor less than night terror attacks. Although dreams can indeed be profitably compared with symptoms, this is only in the larger sense of neurotic symptoms; one does not thereby foreclose the possibility of achieving a unitary conception of dreaming. In contrast, explanations based on the assumption of psychophysiological parallelism tend to be expressed in terms of *individual differences* in susceptibility to regression, on the one hand, or somatization, on the other—Fisher's "symptom" versus Broughton's "disorder of arousal." They are equally "antipsychological" and therefore tend equally to foreclose the possibility of achieving a unitary conception. That is why I insist on anchoring our proposals in a theory of physiological stress based on observations made during waking life.

(3) Reality Testing.

As for the third of Fisher's regressed ego functions, it is difficult to conceive of any observation of the ego during sleep that could confirm the relative state of reality testing. If anything, the results of the buzzer experiment suggest that night terror subjects are no less attuned to external reality during NREM sleep than anxiety-dream subjects are during REM sleep. The only other evidence that could bear on reality testing in prearousal mentation is the frequent observation of night terror subjects that they "knew" they were dreaming. In regard to "the ego's attempt to regain mastery by reestablishing reality testing," Schur (1966) states: "In posttraumatic dreams the dreamer frequently becomes aware of a 'dream within a dream,' of the reassuring fact that he has actually escaped from the trauma" (p. 179; see also the numerous examples cited by Mack [1970]). From what we now know about Stage IV night terrors, however, it is almost certain that this is a postarousal phenomenon.

Fisher seems to argue for regressed prearousal reality testing by analogy to neurotic anxiety. Thus there is "regression from potential or present danger to the traumatic situation," as demonstrated by such postarousal observations as the subject's "calling for mother" and by dreams that "appear to go back to either primal scene experiences or fantasies," for example, or "severe castration wishes and fears, regressively experienced on an oral level" (1970, p. 764). This formulation is based in turn on Schur's (1958)

> assumption that in neurotic anxiety we are dealing with a temporary, partial ego regression. This regression always involves: a) the function of the ego which designates a situation as dangerous, i.e., evaluation of danger. It may also involve: b) the type of reaction to this evaluation. Ego regression tends toward early fixation as does id regression, with the points of fixation depending on genetic and environmental factors [p. 194].

Note the sequence: Regression "toward early fixations" is a "reaction" to a prior "evaluation of danger." If, then, there is regression "to the traumatic situation," this must imply a prior regression in "the function of the ego which designates a situation as dangerous," in reality testing, in other words.

The problem with this formulation is that it is not susceptible to proof, since the only possible measure of the ego's reaction to danger is anxiety. Thus, if there were indeed a prearousal regression in the ego's capacity to evaluate danger, it could be detected only from an increase in autonomic rates evidencing anxiety, although Fisher's very claim for regression is based on a decrease in those rates. In the absence of such proof, then, the inference of prearousal regression is supported solely by the observations of postarousal regression it is meant to explain – the ego is regressed because it is regressed.

But the problem goes even deeper than this, as can be shown by an examination of Schur's (1958) assumption of ego regression. We have already seen that regression "toward early fixations" is a "reaction" to a prior "evaluation of danger." Schur then states that this regression toward early fixations "can re-create a traumatic situation with all its economic implications" (pp. 194–195). He also notes that "the gradual differentiation between potential or present danger, between a situation of present danger and a traumatic situation, is a measure of maturation of reality testing; the failure of such a differentiation is a sign of regression" (p. 196). Thus it is that regressive failure to differentiate between "present danger and a traumatic situation" can lead to "re-creation" of a traumatic situation.

But what is the nature of this regressive failure? In what sense can it be said that the ego fails to "differentiate" between "present danger and a traumatic situation?" The regressive failure to differentiate between present danger and a traumatic situation *must* mean that the ego takes the present danger to *be* the traumatic situation – the traumatic situation must already *exist* in conscious or preconscious thought. On Schur's account, then, this "re-created" traumatic situation—re-created by virtue of the initial regressive "evaluation of danger"—becomes the condition for the "re-creation" of the same traumatic situation by virtue of the subsequent regressive "reaction to this evaluation," by virtue, that is, of the reaction to the *already* "re-created" traumatic situation. The logic is utterly circular: From an anxiety response appropriate to a traumatic situation, Schur infers regression which re-creates the traumatic situation, from which he infers regression which re-creates the traumatic situation; the traumatic situation is re-created because it is re-created. We are left with the idea that traumatic situations recur because the ego cannot differentiate present danger from traumatic situation. But neither can we as observers. That is to say, unless we assume regression, there is no telling if the present danger does not indeed constitute a traumatic situation.

Now I think it is clear that Fisher's explanation in terms of regression represents his alternative to the Freudian conception of repetition compulsion: Regression to the traumatic situation replaces mere. repetition of the traumatic situation. But it is equally clear that when Fisher's regressed ego *mistakes* the present danger for the traumatic situation, when the present danger *is* the traumatic situation, then regression is nothing but repetition by another name. The phenomenon that needs to be explained becomes its own explanation.

The point is an important one because it helps to account for the economic implications of Fisher's thinking. Just as Schur (1958) says, "All through *Inhibitions, Symptoms and Anxiety* Freud distinguishes between anxiety which is 'unwanted,' 'always economically justified,' 'reproduced automatically,' 'created anew out of the economic conditions of the situation' " (pp. 192–193). If, then, anxiety is "created anew" out of the economic conditions of the "merely repeated" traumatic situation, any ostensibly different account must provide a different source of energy. This is to be found in Schur's idea that "ego regression can recreate a traumatic situation with all its economic implications," and more specifically, in Fisher's view of the night terror attack as "a massive eruption of repressed anxiety" (1970, p. 767).

I believe this notion of "repressed anxiety" to be a novel one in the history of psychoanalytic thought. It is true that Freud (1926) repeatedly regarded "the anxiety felt at birth" as "the prototype of an affective state" (p. 162) – of anxiety, that is – but this does not imply that repression of some "whole amount" of anxiety could ever have occurred. Similarly, the idea that anxiety is the reproduction of an "affective state" in accordance with an already "existing mnemic image" (p. 93) suggests, not the storage of anxiety, but the cathexis of a memory trace. Freud's conception of anxiety as a "reaction" to a "situation of non-satisfaction in which the amounts of stimulation arise to an unpleasurable height" (p. 137) is directly contrary to such a view, which can perhaps be understood only in terms of the rejected idea that anxiety is transformed libido (p. 79). On this account, anxiety would be related to libido "in the same kind of way as vinegar is to wine" (Freud, 1905, p. 224n), or rather, as "unconscious vinegar" is to "unconscious wine." On such a basis one might well conclude that pavor nocturnus does not arise beyond the pleasure principle: It would be fueled, or motivated, by repressed anxiety "pressing for discharge."

Before turning to Freud's analysis in *Beyond the Pleasure Principle*, I should like briefly to consider alternative ways in which Fisher's data might be interpreted. His key finding is of course that "the more severe the nightmare the longer the period of Stage IV preceding it, the larger the amount of delta waves and the slower the respiration" (1970, p. 767). Related to this observation is the fact that Stage IV occurs in the first period of sleep "when fatigue is greatest" (p. 767). I have already suggested that lowered heart and respiratory rates can plausibly be interpreted as a physiological stress reaction to preceding threatening dream content. But what of the greater amount of delta sleep?

In this regard, I should like to return to a matter I raised earlier: Fisher's subjects apparently reported much less in the way of nightmare content than do patients in psychoanalysis. Although descriptions of pavor nocturnus nightmares are often meager, Fisher examined a great number of such episodes, of which he presumably presented the most detailed. These do not resemble in many respects the nightmares that pavor nocturnus subjects bring in to psychoanalysis.

I should acknowledge at once that patients in psychoanalysis are profoundly motivated to remember their dreams of the preceding night. They are also probably so motivated to present their dreams in formal dress, so to speak. They have had the time to review them and integrate their experience in a more or less coherent report. Fisher's reports, in contrast, were elicited immediately after his subjects' attacks, in postarousal interviews in which the subjects were apparently still suffering the effects of their attacks. Most of them fell asleep soon after giving their reports, and in a few cases (1974a, p. 334) during the interview itself, sometimes in the middle of a sentence. This hardly argues for their having developed an observing ego. Fisher (1974b) acknowledges, moreover, that "in four of six subjects with the most reported content, aspects of the sleep laboratory occurred in over 50 per cent of the reports. Therefore, this has not been a study of night terror content in general but in a particular situation, that is, the subjects slept in a laboratory" (pp. 186–187). The artificiality of the laboratory setting, I submit, might account for the difference in content between his reports and those obtained in clinical psychoanalysis. Other admissions of that artificiality were made in the 1970 study:

> In general, in the laboratory, the motility aspect of the
> Stage IV nightmare was not seen because contact was
> established with the subjects very quickly after they
> screamed and the confusional state thus interrupted.
> The presence of the attached electrodes may also be a
> factor in restraining motility [p. 754; also 1974a, p.
> 331].

Note that the confusional state was "interrupted," consistent
with my view that Fisher's subjects were still in the throes of
stupor. Again:

> Many of our subjects reported that they had severe
> nightmares at home with screaming and vocalization,
> would awaken with heart beating in marked anxiety,
> but in the laboratory their nightmares were much less
> severe. [To which Fisher appended this footnote.]
> Broughton made a similar observation (1968). Quite
> probably the reduction in severity has to do with the
> fact that someone is present and in communication
> with the subject all night, thus reducing separation
> anxiety which plays an important role in nightmares
> [p. 757].

My point is simply that given the artificiality of the laboratory situation that Fisher employed, it is doubtful that his
reports give an accurate picture of the mental content associated with night terror attacks.

The implications of this are considerable. One of the
bases for Fisher's (1970) description of the night terror as a
"symptom" is the following:

> REM anxiety causing arousal emerges out of a com-
> plex, prolonged dream which, on the average, had

been in progress for 20 minutes. The NREM arousal nightmare, on the contrary, is a sudden, instantaneous, cataclysmic event associated with a single scene and taking place simultaneously with it [p. 773].

But if the evidence for this was obtained from still "symptomatic" subjects, from subjects in the throes of stupor, then we cannot be surprised that the "cataclysmic event" was associated with a "single scene." If Fisher were to respond that these events were also not associated with preceding autonomic change evidencing anxiety, it need only be pointed out that neither was such autonomic change associated with 12 of the 20 arousals he classifies as REM anxiety dreams (p. 758). Indeed, it is difficult to see on what basis he has determined that such dreams "had been in progress for 20 minutes," since the only basis for such a determination could have been the measures of autonomic activation that showed no change in the 12 "exceptional" REM anxiety dreams. Perhaps he means that the "unexceptional" eight had been in progress for 20 minutes. This might also be the time to point out the illegitimacy of explaining the "exceptions" in terms of a "desomatization mechanism" in REM sleep (pp. 770–772). Once again, an observation has served as the basis for its own explanation: Some REM anxiety dreams are desomatized because they are desomatized.

In the light of these considerations, I suggest that we might plausibly interpret the longer duration of Stage IV sleep before more severe arousals as a measure not of regression but of a developing nightmare—all the more so because "mental activity, generally less dreamlike and more secondary process in nature, has been shown to go on during nondreaming sleep, so that the mind seems never to rest" (Fisher, 1970, p. 749). We might then attribute the fact that such arousals occur in the first period of sleep to the evidence that "mental content from NREM sleep" is more "concerned with recent events of the preceding day" (1974b, p. 176). I suggest that, at the very least, these inferences are no less plausible than Fisher's inference of regression. As I shall show in Chapter 3, neither do they give rise to the various contradictions I have laid to Fisher's interpretation of the data. There too I shall demonstrate their congruence with a conception of the posttraumatic dream as a manifestation of the repetition compulsion.

3

Trauma and
the Repetition Compulsion

T he cornerstone of Freud's argument in *Beyond the Pleasure Principle* (1920) was the observation that "dreams occurring in traumatic neuroses have the characteristic of repeatedly bringing the patient back into the situation of his accident, a situation from which he wakes up in another fright." Of this he remarked:

> Anyone who accepts it as something self-evident that their dreams should put them back at night into the situation that caused them to fall ill has misunderstood the nature of dreams. It would be more in harmony with their nature if they showed the patient pictures from his healthy past or of the cure for which he hopes [p. 13].

These repetitive dreams, in other words, did not seem to serve the purpose of fulfilling wishes. What purpose did they serve?

To answer this question Freud turned to "the method of working employed by the mental apparatus in one of its earliest *normal* activities, children's play, specifically, the game of disappearance and return staged by a one-and-a-half-year-old boy in relation to his mother's occasionally leaving him for a few hours. Freud noted that "the child cannot possibly have felt his mother's departure as something agreeable or even indifferent," so that his repetition of the experience as a game looked to be an exception to the pleasure principle, the more so because as a rule one only witnessed its "first act," the disappearance. Freud then proposed that the game might be attributed "to an instinct for mastery that was acting independently of whether the memory was itself pleasurable or not. . . . At the outset [the boy] was in a *passive* situation—he was overpowered by the experience; but, by repeating it, unpleasurable though it was, as a game, he took on an *active* part." Repetition, then, might serve an "impulse to work over in the mind some overpowering experience so as to make oneself master of it" (pp. 14–16).

Freud's third example of unpleasurable repetition came from the analytic situation, wherein the neurotic patient is "obliged to *repeat* the repressed material as a contemporary experience" in the transference neurosis. This "compulsion to repeat" did not contradict the pleasure principle to the extent that it could be explained in terms of previous satisfactions of repressed instinctual impulses, felt by the ego as unpleasure. But, Freud continued, "we come now to a new and remarkable fact, namely, that the compulsion to repeat also recalls from the past experiences which include no possibility of pleasure, and which can never, even long ago, have brought satisfaction even to instinctual impulses which have since been repressed." Significantly, this *neurotic* compulsion to repeat differed "in no way" from cases in which a normal person—who has "never shown any signs of dealing with a neurotic conflict by producing symptoms"— "appears to have a *passive* experience, over which he has no influence, but in which he meets with a repetition of the same fatality (pp. 18–22). By inference, then, neither did the neurotic compulsion to repeat differ from children's normal repetition play insofar as such play reflected the subject's original passivity in the face of the underlying unpleasurable experience. Nor, for that matter, did it differ from the dreams of posttraumatic neuroses in which the passively experienced "situation in which the trauma occurred" is repeated in the subject's sleep. Finally, in the sense that "the patient behaves in a purely infantile fashion" (p. 36) the compulsion to repeat appears to be a neurotic manifestation of "the method of working employed by the mental apparatus in one of its earliest normal activities," in children's play, which is to say, a relatively *primitive* method of working. The significance for Freud that these repetitive phenomena arose in *normal* as well as abnormal behavior, and represented one of the *earliest* activities of the mind, was revealed in his ultimate willingness "to assume that there really does exist in the mind a compulsion to repeat" (p. 22), which "seems more primitive, more elementary, more instinctual than the pleasure principle which it over-rides" (p. 23). For Freud, that is, the compulsion to repeat was "more instinctual" *because* it was "primitive" and "elementary."

It remained for him to establish the relationship between the original passivity in the face of the trauma, which he had held common to all four cases, and the function of mastery that he had attributed to children's play. In children's play this connection was hinted at in the idea that repetition of the unpleasurable experience as a game gave evidence of the child's "taking an active part" in relation to it. By virtue of an "instinct for mastery," the child seemed to be "making happen" the unpleasure that had at first merely "happened" to him. The success of the game from a developmental standpoint was indicated in Freud's comment that "above all" the boy "never cried when his mother left him for a few hours" (p. 14).

But the relationship of activity to mastery was not explained, and we must turn to Freud's earlier distinction between "anxiety" and "fright" for clarification: " 'Anxiety' describes a particular state of expecting the danger or preparing for it, even though it may be an unknown one. . . . 'Fright,' however, is the name we give to the state a person gets into when he has run into danger without being prepared for it" (p. 12). Anxiety may thus be seen to represent the "active part" the subject takes toward danger — "preparing for it" — while fright would indicate his passivity, or failure to have "prepared for it." Accordingly, if "at the outset" the child "was in a passive situation," unprepared for the danger of his mother's leaving, then the activity of the game — his making unpleasure "happen" — might demonstrate his developing capacity to prepare for that danger, his development of anxiety in regard to it. In the absence of abstract thought, the symbolic mechanism of the game constitutes a mental preparation for danger.

To explain how this development came about — how an instinctual compulsion to repeat led from original passivity, or unpreparedness, to mastery, or preparedness — Freud turned to cases from which such development was absent, specifically, the dreams of the traumatic neuroses. Passivity was defined in metapsychological terms as the "lack of hypercathexis of the systems that would be the first to receive" the traumatic stimulus (p. 31) and mastery as the "binding" of that stimulus (p. 31). The connection between passivity and mastery as thus metapsychologically defined was stated in the following:

From the present case . . . we infer that a system
which is itself highly cathected is capable of taking up
an additional stream of fresh inflowing energy and of
converting it into quiescent cathexis, that is, of
binding it psychically. The higher the system's own
quiescent cathexis, the greater seems to be its binding
force; conversely, therefore, the lower its cathexis, the
less capacity will it have for taking up inflowing
energy [p. 30].

What happened in the case of trauma—when "excitations
from outside" were "powerful enough to break through the
protective shield" against stimuli (p. 29) was that "owing to
their low cathexis" the systems that would be "the first to
receive" the traumatic stimuli were "not in a good position
for binding the inflowing amounts of excitation" (p. 31) not
in a "good position," that is, for "converting it into quiescent
cathexis." The problem then became one of "mastering the
amounts of stimulus which have broken in and of binding
them, in the psychical sense, so that they can then be
disposed of (p. 30).

Freud then restated his distinction between anxiety and
fright in metapsychological terms: Fright was

caused by lack of any preparedness for anxiety, including lack of hypercathexis of the systems that
would be the first to receive the stimulus . . . preparedness for anxiety and the hypercathexis of the
receptive systems constitute the last line of defense of
the shield against stimuli. In the case of quite a
number of traumas, the difference between systems
that are unprepared and systems that are well prepared through being hypercathected may be a deci-
sive factor in the determining outcome [pp. 31–32].

(I am, of course, interpreting "preparedness for anxiety" here to mean "preparedness for danger," so as to avoid the unintelligible "preparedness for the state of expecting the danger or preparing for it"; see also Strachey's footnote 1, p. 13). From a metapsychological standpoint, then, in order for anxiety or a preparedness for danger to develop, systems with low cathexis had to become "hypercathected" so as to be able to convert inflowing energy into quiescent cathexis. The source of energy for this hypercathexis remained obscure, however. On the one hand, it seemed to be provided by other systems:

> Cathectic energy is summoned from all sides to provide sufficiently high cathexes of energy in the environs of the breach. An "anticathexis" on a grand scale is set up, for whose benefit all other psychical systems are impoverished, so that the remaining psychical functions are extensively paralyzed or reduced [p. 30].

This seems to account for the pleasure principle's being "put out of action" (p. 29) and for the "comprehensive general enfeeblement and disturbance of the mental capacities" observed in traumatic neuroses (p. 12). It also accounts for repression (p. 11). On the other hand, this provision of energy could not have a lasting effect if only because the original stimulus arose again in the subject's dreams in such a way that he woke up "in another fright," demonstrating that preparedness for danger, or hypercathexis of the relevant systems, had not developed. Such a permanent expenditure of energy, moreover, giving rise to "general enfeeblement and disturbance of the mental capacities," could not be regarded as successful from the standpoint of adaptation.

Some other process, then, had to explain the development of the hypercathexis of these systems. This was repetition:

It is not in the service of [the pleasure principle] that the dreams of patients suffering from traumatic neurosis lead them back with such regularity to the situation in which the trauma occurred. We may assume, rather, that dreams are here helping to carry out another task, which must be accomplished before the dominance of the pleasure principle can even begin. These dreams are endeavouring to master the stimulus retrospectively, by developing the anxiety whose omission was the cause of the traumatic neurosis [p. 32].

That is to say, these dreams were developing "the preparedness for danger," or hypercathexis of the relevant systems, whose "omission was the cause of the traumatic neurosis." On this account, then, the evidence for *lack* of preparedness—repetition—has been used to explain how preparedness develops. In the absence of any other explanatory construct, the compulsion to repeat must be regarded as leading from unpreparedness to preparedness by way of unpreparedness, from passivity to mastery by way of passivity.

I believe that the missing explanatory construct is available in Freudian theory, but not in *Beyond the Pleasure Principle* (1920). It appears, or, rather, is implied, in *Inhibitions, Symptoms and Anxiety* (1926); and if I have gone at some length into the cul-de-sac of Freud's metapsychological speculations in the former work, it is because I believe those speculations to be compatible with the construct to which I have referred.

This construct is the necessary basis for Freud's (1926) conception of signal anxiety, whereby

the ego subjects itself to anxiety as a sort of inoculation, submitting to a slight attack of the illness in order to escape its full strength. It vividly imagines the danger-situation, as it were, with the unmistakable purpose of restricting that distressing experience to a mere indication, a signal [p. 162].

In signal anxiety, in other words, the subject has developed the capacity to utilize his states of tension as signals of danger. *This must mean that he has acquired the ability to attribute meaning to those states of tension, where such ability was absent in the past.* This ability, then, is the precondition for the movement from unpreparedness, or passivity, to preparedness, or mastery.

That this is what Freud meant can be shown by an examination of the one certain case in which anxiety was not used as a signal: the trauma of birth. Thus:

In the act of birth there is a real danger to life. We know what this means objectively; but in a psychological sense it says nothing at all to us. The danger of birth has as yet no psychical content. We cannot possibly suppose that the foetus has any sort of knowledge that there is a possibility of its life being destroyed. It can only be aware of some vast disturbance in the economy of its narcissistic libido [p. 135].

Now compare this situation with the

transition from the automatic and involuntary fresh appearance of anxiety to the intentional reproduction of anxiety as a signal of danger. . . . When the infant has found out by experience that an external, perceptible object can put an end to the dangerous situation which is reminiscent of birth, the content of the danger it fears is displaced from the economic situation on to the condition which determined that situation, viz., the loss of the object. It is the absence of the mother that is now the danger; and as soon as that danger arises the infant gives the signal of anxiety, before the dreaded economic situation has set in: [pp. 137–138].

Note that the content of the danger is "displaced" from the economic situation "reminiscent of birth" onto "the condition which determined that situation." But if the danger at birth had "no psychical content," if the foetus could "only be aware of some vast disturbance in the economy of its narcissistic libido," this "displacement" must imply that an economic disturbance which, as it were, originally signified nothing but itself has come to *refer* to the condition that determined it. In other words, the economic disturbance has acquired meaning. This meaning, then—the danger of "the absence of the mother"—is the precondition for the infant's giving the signal of anxiety "before the dreaded economic situation has set in."

I think that if we adopt this interpretation, Freud's use of repetition as an explanatory construct in *Beyond the Pleasure Principle* becomes comprehensible. From everything he has said, it is obvious that the capacity to attribute meaning to one's own states of tension is acquired by experience:

Preparedness for anxiety, instead of being at its maximum immediately after birth and then slowly decreasing, does not emerge till later, as mental development proceeds . . . [p. 136]; man seems not to have been endowed, or to have been endowed to only a very small degree, with an instinctive recognition of the dangers that threaten him from without [p. 168].

As we have seen, it is only when "the infant has found out by experience that an external, perceptible object can put an end to the dangerous situation" that "displacement" to the condition that determined that situation occurs. This "dangerous situation," moreover, "must for the infant be analogous to the experience of being born — must be a repetition of the situation of danger" (p. 137). We may well wonder how this capacity is "learned" from experience by an infant incapable of becoming conscious of the *absence* of tension, but it is difficult to conceive of its acquisition *without* experience, that is to say, without repetition. It may be that such a capacity develops in the context of the child's interactions with his mother. Spitz's (1945) well-known study of infants separated from their mothers at birth demonstrated, among many other things, that such infants showed slowed reactions to external stimuli. Harlow et al. (1965, p. 94) established that monkeys reared in isolation from their mothers did not defend themselves when attacked, suggesting that at least the "fight" half of the "fight-flight" complex may need to be "triggered" by interaction with the mother. At all events, we may fairly conclude that when Freud attributed the repetitive behavior of patients in the transference neurosis to the evidence that "no lesson has been learnt from the old experience" of unpleasure (1920, p. 21), he meant that such patients had failed to develop the capacity to attribute meaning to their states of tension and that this was the "task" which "must be accomplished before the dominance of the pleasure principle can even begin" (p. 32).

Let us now reconsider Freud's formulations in *Beyond the Pleasure Principle* with a view to determining their compatibility with the construct I have described. If this construct is the necessary basis for signal anxiety, whereby the ego submits "to a slight attack of the illness in order to escape its full strength," then it must also be the necessary basis for the "preparedness" of the system that would be the "first to receive" the traumatic stimulus, the system *Pcpt.-Cs.* Of this system Freud (1920) remarked: "The main purpose of the *reception* of stimuli is to discover the direction and nature of the external stimuli; and for that it is enough to take small specimens of the external world to sample it in small quantities" (p. 27). And: "It is characteristic of [the sense organs] that they deal only with very small quantities of external stimulation and only take in *samples* of the external world" (p. 28). The sampling/signal conception had, of course, a long history in Freud's thought. In *The Interpretation of Dreams* (1900) it is stated that thinking must aim "at restricting the development of affect in thought-activity to the minimum required for acting as a signal" (p. 602). The idea is that "small specimens of the external world" are sufficient to bring about states of tension giving evidence of "the direction and nature of the external stimuli." But these affective signals or "slight attacks of the illness" can only develop in an organism capable of attributing meaning to its states of tension, to its affect. This capacity, then, can be conceived in terms of a developing ability to *abstract* from such states of tension to the "direction and nature of the external stimuli," a matter at which Freud hinted when he noted that "our abstract idea of time seems to be wholly derived from the method of working of the system *Pcpt.-Cs.* and to correspond to a perception on its own part of that method of working" (1920, pp. 27–28). Here he seemed to be referring to a "method of working" in which the organism abstracted from the sample to the "nature of the external stimuli." But the nature of the sample itself could not be determined without an original abstraction from the state of tension to which it gave rise. That is why Freud character- ized the child's game of disappearance and return as "activ- ity": By "making happen" the tension that had at first merely "happened" to him, the child was presumably learning this critical method of active sampling.

We may also be closer to an understanding of Freud's conception of binding. In his discussion of the transference neuroses, he noted that "the patient behaves in a purely infantile fashion and thus shows us that the repressed memory traces of his primaeval experiences are not present in him in a bound state and are indeed in a sense incapable of obeying the secondary process" [p. 36].

In this regard, it was easy for Freud "to identify the primary psychical process with Breuer's freely mobile cathexis and the secondary process with changes in his bound or tonic cathexis" (p. 34). That is to say, "in the unconscious," where the primary process prevails, "cathexis can easily be completely transferred, displaced and condensed. Such treatment, however, could produce only invalid results if it were applied to preconscious material . . ." (p. 34). Now, we have already seen that "the transition from the automatic and involuntary fresh appearance of anxiety to the intentional reproduction of anxiety as a signal" requires a "displacement" from the economic situation to "the condition which determined that situation." But if this displacement took place under the influence of the primary process, where "cathexis can easily be transferred, displaced and condensed," it would not produce the meaning that is the necessary basis for signal anxiety, it would produce "only invalid results," a displacement, as it were, from the economic situation to the unconscious kitchen sink. Thus it is "the task of the higher strata of the mental apparatus to bind the instinctual excitation reaching the primary process (pp. 34–35). That is to say, it is their task to bring about a displacement from such "excitations" to the "condition that determined them." When such excitations thus come to "obey the secondary process," we can interpret the metapsychological process involved as literally requiring the "binding" of an inner state of tension to an external condition, or what is the same thing, a relatively permanent disposition to displace it to that condition, and no other. Similarly, the quality of quiescence attributed to bound psychic energy can now be interpreted in terms of the stability of meaning attributed to that inner state. Mastery and binding would thus be synonyms for the attribution of meaning to one's own states of tension, without which preparedness for danger could not develop.

All of this, of course, implies a beginning coordination of the subject with reality before the dominance of the pleasure principle could even begin, and therefore before its modification in the reality principle. This should not surprise us, however, inasmuch as the pleasure principle is inconceivable in terms other than a *subjective* awareness of one's own states of tension as unpleasurable, and it is precisely the development of subjectivity that is being described by Freud in his conception of displacement from states of tension to an external condition. Moreover, to the extent that this development depends on the infant's finding out "by experience that an external, perceptible object can put an end to the dangerous situation" of tension, it requires a "match" between the infant's expression of his need and a gratifying external reality. This does not mean that a wish for such gratifications cannot subsequently result in conflict with an external depriving, or punishing, reality such as to bring about the familiar primary process displacements of dreams and the compromise formations of the symptom. Hence, the classical basis for the development of the reality principle in the experience of conflict remains intact. So too does the dominance of the unconscious and the primary process in the neurotic resolution of ambivalence in symptom formation. These events, however, must now be regarded as following a developmental process that cannot be considered subjectively motivated by unconscious wishes, or, put another way, must be considered motivated by objective biological states to which a gratifying reality is, in optimal circumstances, coordinated. The relative lack of such coordination will result not only in greater or lesser degrees of trauma, but in a relative failure to develop the capacity to attribute meaning to one's own states of tension, a type of faulty learning. Such a failure will issue in frank repetitions of apparent wishes that do not conform to external reality and whose expression will differ from those of classical wishes in displaying little of the ambiguity characteristic of conflict. That is to say, these "wishes" can be detected by virtue of their unreality, their not having been distorted by primary process mechanisms, and their expression in outright repetition rather than in symptom formation.

Perhaps I can clarify these matters with regard to Schur's (1966) critique of Freud's analysis in *Beyond the Pleasure Principle*. In making his case that repetitive behavior in the transference neurosis could not be considered subjectively motivated by unconscious wishes, Freud had laid particular stress on the unreality of his patients' infantile wishes, none of which "can have produced pleasure in the past" (p. 21). These wishes, "incompatible with reality and with the inadequate stage of development which the child has reached" (p. 20) can never have produced the desired "match" with external reality simply because they ran against the objective facts of the infant's biological life. Thus, Freud's emphasis on "the child's sexual researches, on which limits are imposed by his physical development," and on his "attempt to make a baby" (p. 21). In this regard, Schur states:

> But can we not say that *most* sexual, aggressive, and omnipotent fantasies, even of later life, *never* meet with satisfaction? This certainly applies to most of the wishes which represent instinctual danger, elicit signal anxiety, and are subject to repression or other defenses. Such wishes, which are completely distorted in dreams, frequently result in anxiety and can be detected in symptom formation [p. 183].

Schur is describing the characteristic fate of the classical wish in the face of conflict. But he seems to have missed Freud's point that certain of these "wishes" result not in symptom formation but in outright repetition, implying failure to elicit signal anxiety and ensuing regression. In fact, he attributes such repetition to just such a classical wish, both in posttraumatic dreams and in the transference neurosis:

> According to my interpretation, the repetition of traumatic events in dreams represents—apart from the gratification of various id derivatives and superego "demands"—the ego's unconscious wish to *undo* the traumatic situation. This cannot be done without reliving the latter in endless variation. The resulting anxiety is an ego response to danger, no different from the result of other anxiety-provoking dreams, in which the wish represents a forbidden instinctual (sexual or aggressive) demand [p. 178].

Schur is arguing, then, that repetition in posttraumatic dreams need not be attributed to a compulsion to repeat "beyond the pleasure principle," but can be regarded as motivated by a subjective wish on the part of the ego to "undo" the traumatic situation.

In regard to this interpretation, I think we must first ask whether it is true that the "resulting anxiety" of the posttraumatic dream is "no different from the result of other anxiety-provoking dreams." Surely it is different in a quantitative sense, inasmuch as the posttraumatic dreamer, according to Freud, "wakes up in another fright," or what he later called "automatic" or "full-blown" anxiety (1926). This was, of course, one of the facts that led Freud to take up the dreams of posttraumatic neurosis in the first place. Now, as Schur suggests, anxiety can arise in response to a situation of danger or to a wish whose fulfillment would bring about a situation of danger. In either case, the ego's response is to a threatened repetition of a previous traumatic event. If it is indeed the case that "the repetition of traumatic events in dreams represents . . . the ego's unconscious wish to undo the traumatic situation," then Schur must explain why it is that full-blown anxiety does not develop in *all* anxiety dreams, inasmuch as in order for the traumatic situation to be undone, it has to be "re-lived in endless variation." That is to say, if anxiety results from the threatened repetition of a previous traumatic situation, and if all such dreams evidence anxiety, then all such dreams must represent an unconscious wish on the part of the ego to undo a traumatic situation. To maintain otherwise would require us to conceive of the ego as wishing to undo one traumatic situation and not the other, wishing to undo the episode that led to shellshock but not the episode that led to the overwhelming threat of castration. It is no answer to this to suppose that a conflict exists between the sexual wish that led to the threat of castration and the ego's wish to undo the situation, since both wishes are ultimately motivations to "relive" the situation in which gratification led to danger. At the same time, moreover, the ego that is so motivated to relive the danger situation must also be motivated to make that situation "not to have happened," Freud's (1926) definition of undoing, an absurdity comparable to viewing the id as wanting and not wanting exclusive sexual possession of mother. Schur is indeed careful to avoid directly stating that the ego wishes to relive the danger situation, for the obvious reason that such a formulation would constitute, on the face of it, a departure from standard psychoanalytic thinking. Thus it is always: The ego's wish is the undoing of the traumatic event. "This cannot be attempted without the recreation of the trauma" (p. 178), or "the ego's unconscious wish [is] to undo the traumatic situation. This cannot be done without reliving the latter in endless variation" (p. 178). Yet the whole point of Schur's argument against the idea that traumatic repetitions arise beyond the pleasure principle is that such repetitions *must* be motivated by a wish. Thus, whether it is couched in terms of a wish to undo or a wish to relive, Schur's formulation must take the form of a wish *to repeat*. In this sense, his wish to undo is a wish to repeat in sheep's clothing.

Nor do I think it possible for Schur to account for the facts of development in terms of this formulation. It is impossible to conceive of signal anxiety—the *sampling* of a danger situation—as being brought to bear on an opposing wish to *relive* the situation. Any model of signal anxiety thus based on Schur's conception would require us to view the same ego as *permitting* the satisfaction of its wish to relive the situation, thereby to *bring about* the feared situation of danger, thereby to *avoid* the reliving of the danger situation, with absurdities no less palpable than those noted earlier. If, finally, it is impossible to conceive of signal anxiety in terms of such a conception, it is similarly impossible to conceive of repression and symptom formation in terms of it. Surely it makes more sense to attribute the repetitive phenomena of posttraumatic dreams and the transference neurosis to factors "beyond the pleasure principle" than to a wish that cannot be made to behave as do the other wishes in psychoanalytic experience.

I believe we may now profitably compare Freud's examples of "wishes" that do not conform to reality with those provided by Schur in his discussion of "impervious resistance to working through": "the frequent experience of women in the last phases of their analysis who go through a period of depression when they are forced to realize that analysis will not equip them with a penis," and women who "realize, too late, that the right time had passed for finding a proper mate and bearing children" (p. 188). In their unreality and frankness of expression, these "wishes" are not only consistent with the examples supplied by Freud, but also with the idea that they have never been subject to conflict in the classical sense. They arise in obedience to a compulsion to repeat, in the service of correcting a developmental failure to attribute appropriate meaning to a state of tension. Such is the logic of Freud's argument that, in the absence of education similar to that originally provided by the optimal mother, these dispositions will persist unchanged over time, as "signals" of a need to experience an external reality coordinated to an objective state of tension.

Traumatic dreams, then, are not produced by psychic conflict. Contrary to Schur's claim, the evidence now suggests that they do not involve wishes such as "are completely distorted in dreams"—they do not involve, that is, attempts at the resolution of ambivalence in unconsciously chosen pieces of ambiguity. The lack of primary-process distortion on which I laid so much stress earlier can now be seen to be consonant with the frankness of expression characteristic of the "unreal wishes" of the transference neurosis. To the extent that these dreams do exhibit aspects of unreality, they should be taken as evidence of relative failure to attribute appropriate meaning to a state of tension. To put this another way, not all such cases can be traced back to a lack of coordination with an original gratifying reality. In the case of recent traumatization, we should expect to find that the night terror attacks of persons who have not suffered severe trauma in infancy will display less unreality than do those of subjects who have been so traumatized. The former persons, in whom the capacity to attribute meaning to states of tension has been securely established, will, however, experience night terror repetitions to the extent that the recent state of tension has not been mastered. In the absence of preparedness for danger, the subject will revert—indeed, regress—to the method of working employed by the mental apparatus in its earliest efforts at mastery. His dreams will thus persist until adaptation to the consequences of the trauma has occurred—that is, until signal anxiety can be brought to bear on the memory of the traumatic situation. In this sense, repression by means of signal anxiety is the necessary precondition for further adaptation to the trauma by means of the development of an intellectual under- standing of the situation that led up to it, in sum, the necessary precondition for thought.

Seen in this light, Broughton's (1968) discovery that night terror attacks occur in Stage IV sleep is not as aston- ishing as it once seemed. When such attacks are viewed as repetitive efforts to establish a beginning coordination be- tween a state of tension and external reality, it makes sense that they should occur in a phase of sleep that yields dream reports "less bizarre, less affective, more like ordinary thought—or secondary-process thinking in psychoanalytic terminology—and more concerned with the contemporary lives of the subjects" (quoted by Mack, 1970, p. 192). It may thus be that NREM sleep is devoted to the resolution of the very problem Freud addressed in *Beyond the Pleasure Princi- ple*: the attribution of meaning to one's own states of tension. REM phases, in contrast, would be concerned with the resolution of problems involving ambivalence, which would account for the greater appearance of primary process dis- tortion in dream reports elicited from them. This interpreta- tion, I might add, supports the views of Rapaport (1960) and Holt (1967) that the secondary process develops not out of the primary process, but in parallel with it, from an original "undifferentiated matrix" (Rapaport, 1960, p. 234). Nor does it result in the numerous contradictions I have laid to the regression explanation of the same material. On that expla- nation, as we have seen, regression must lead both to the appearance of primary-process thinking and a weakening of repression when a weakening of repression would be expected to result in lesser appearance of primary process. At the same time, the regression explanation contradicts the evidence for just such a lesser appearance of primary process thoughts in night terror attacks. My formulation, in contrast, explains this evidence in terms of the distinct form of mental activity represented by NREM ideation, which serves the function of mastery. Until such mastery occurs—until, that is, the development of repression by signal anxiety—we should not expect primary process thought to appear. Similarly, my formulation accounts in a more coherent way for the results of the buzzer experiment: The greater than usual responsiveness to the environment of night terror subjects during NREM sleep would reflect a mental state concerned with making accurate, nonsubjective judgments of external reality events.

For Freud, of course, the basis for the repetition compulsion lay in the "urge inherent in organic life *to restore an earlier state of things*" (1920, p. 36)—in the death instinct. We have seen that the repetition compulsion does indeed serve mental activity more primitive and elementary than that associated with conflict; but whether this supports the claim that such repetitions can be attributed to an instinct—or, for that matter, a "death instinct" that is opposed to a "life instinct"—is arguable. My own preference is for a unitary conception of biological and mental activity. The evidence I cited earlier concerning the initial signal function of the physiological reaction to stress may provide a basis for just such a unitary conception, as opposed to Freud's dualistic one. In Chapter 5 I shall elaborate this conception in terms of what I shall describe as the "teleonomic principle" of biological activity.

4

Reparative Mastery

T he repetitive "unreal wishes" I described in the preceding chapter, however maladaptive they may be in the
long run, serve the immediate purpose of maintaining a
pseudointegratedness of the ego by means of which the
patient seemingly functions as an autonomous personality in
the face of disorganizing tension. Because they thus serve to
"repair" breaches in the ego, I view them as instances of
what I have previously termed "reparative mastery." Such
"wishes" always betoken developmental failure in the resolution of the symbiotic relationship of infancy: When deprivations of mothering result in severe trauma in infancy, ego
functions whereby the infant recognizes himself as distinct
from his surroundings and the agent of his own well-being
do not develop to a degree sufficient to permit mastery of
disorganizing states of tension. In their absence, to whatever

extent, such states of tension will be attributed by the patient neither to a need for symbiotic gratification nor, still less, to the developmental insufficiency that resulted from the frustration of that need, but rather to an objective condition of his existence that can be rectified only by what amounts to, but cannot be recognized as, a renunciation of his subjectivity. When Schur's patient wishes that analysis would equip her with a penis (1966, p. 168), she wishes ultimately, meaninglessly, not to be herself. She wishes to exist in a state of undifferentiated union with the analyst that admits no distinction between self and non-self, a state as impossible of being experienced subjectively as was that of symbiotic union with the mother, before the onset of subjectivity. This unrecognizable renunciation of subjectivity, to whatever extent it exists, is a renunciation of personal agency to that same extent. The patient's state of tension, which is his to master, is rather to be mastered by another, who performs precisely those functions that the patient cannot perform himself and that were originally performed by the symbiotic mother. Gratification of symbiotic dependency needs thus serves at once to reduce the disorganizing state of tension and to maintain the pseudointegratedness of the ego by preserving the symbiotic bond in fantasy. Needless to say, these developmental failures will vary in degree to the same extent as the episodes of trauma that gave them rise. As Freud wrote in 1940, "No human individual is spared such traumatic experiences; none escapes the repressions to which they give rise" (p. 185). This view agrees with my own that repetitive phenomena in treatment are expressions of ubiquitous biotraumata whose mastery, by repression proper, accounts for the phenomenal development of the human mind and whose failure to be mastered—whose persistence in primal repression—lies at the very heart of mental disorder, of schizophrenia in cases of overwhelming trauma, of neurosis in cases of lesser but still morbid traumatization marked by attempts at reparative mastery. In the latter instance, the conflicts of later stages of development will be superimposed on the original developmental failure.

The most egregious examples of reparative mastery occur with respect to irrational wishes on the part of the patient for protection by the analyst against death. In *The Interpretation of Dreams* Freud (1900) wrote: "The fear of death has no meaning to a child [and] children know nothing of the horror of corruption, of freezing in the ice-cold grave, of the terrors of eternal nothingness" (p. 254). In his attempt to base mental phenomena either on instinctual needs emerging from the unconscious or on prototypical previous situations, Freud (1926) found in the instance of death neither one nor the other:

> The unconscious seems to contain nothing that could give any content to the concept of the annihilation of life . . . [and] nothing resembling death can ever have been experienced; or if it has, as in fainting, it has left no observable traces behind [pp. 129–130].

Nevertheless, Anna Freud (1960) reports that children at the age of two or three already have developed some idea of death, and adult patients in my own practice frequently express fears for their own deaths. These fears, I should say, amount to a renunciation of the subjectively alien.

I began to provide interpretations to this effect in severe cases of long duration that had not had the success one would have wished. All these cases were marked by stubborn clinging to the analytic situation and impasses in the resolution of the transference neurosis. The effect of the interpretations was, in most cases, dramatic. Interpretation of transference as irrational protection against death elicited marked depression, with feelings of emptiness and despair, paralysis of activity, and an often alarming dimming of the sensorium, felt as haziness and lasting for weeks; this was usually followed by flaring up of symbiotic fantasies whose interpretation opened the way for belated mastery of individuation. All these cases, I might add, were characterized by severe disturbances in the early mother-child relationship.

CASE 1

A 38-year-old married male, a compulsive character plagued by insomnia and frequent pavor nocturnus dreams, hypochondriacal fears, and working difficulties, needed perverse fantasies to reach gratification in his sexual relations and to fall asleep, among them the fantasy of being sat upon and breathed into. His childhood had been replete with traumas. In his infancy, his parents, who preferred traveling around the world, had frequently given him up to the care of others, the first time when he was only six months old. Later he was brought up in a boarding school. He had had several severe diseases that were traumatogenic because of the absence of his parents. His perverse fantasies could be traced back to reminiscences of a tonsillectomy and a narcosis.

The fantasy of being sat upon and breathed into enabled him in only insufficient degree to enjoy sex while undoing castration anxiety. On the oedipal level it meant incestuous feminine identification and in terms of pregenital regression being shit into and destroyed; both are undone by symbiotic fusion via respiratory (and oral) incorporation of the mother.

The working through of his conflicts on the oedipal level and their reflection in the transference neurosis brought improvement, but no definite change in his perverse withdrawal. Finally, transference material referring to a wish to get from the analyst a magical formula for the stone of the sages elicited the interpretation that he conceived of analysis as protection against fear of death and that no one was able to protect him against inevitable death. This interpretation effected a surprising turn. It brought into analysis his permanent fears of dying, manifested in his hypochondriacal complaints; his desperate struggle with the fear of nothingness in the beginning of his latency period; and his wish to stay forever in analysis.

His demands for a magic formula from the analyst meant that he could give up his perversion only when the analyst provided him with another formula against death. The insight that the analyst was incapable of this plunged him into a deep depression. His hyperactivity in his work and in his hobbies, which helped him in his withdrawal from the family, turned into feelings of being utterly helpless, of living in a haze, of dissolution of his identity. This induced a regression to symbiotic fantasies of oral incorporation of his wife and the analyst, and tremendous rage against both. Consistent working through of the symbiotic material led to an improvement of separation-individuation so deficient under the traumatic conditions of his childhood. Simultaneously his symptoms diminished consistently; his object relations to his wife and to his colleagues changed. He experienced love as never before. The analysis could be terminated.

CASE 2

A male lawyer, who presented masochistic, feminine character trends and acting out of perverse fantasies of being penetrated in anal masturbation, could not keep a job. Quarreling with his superiors, gambling, and drinking had the goal of provoking punishment. His marriage was unhappy. He detested his wife. His obviously psychopathic

mother, whom he described as an indolent, dirty woman, "a
piece of shit, nothing but a bad smelling vagina," had
resented and neglected her many children. As an infant he
had refused contact with her and had slept for years in the
bed of his black nanny. His mother secretly drank and
smoked, heavy sins in the puritanical family. Very seductive,
she used to expose herself before him; he observed her
masturbating and frequently witnessed intercourse between
his parents. In nightmares, both father and mother appeared
as ghoulish monsters. At the center of his relationship with
his puritanical father, during his latency and adolescence,
was a relentless struggle over smoking. Because of it, the
harsh and very religious father, after long sermons, used to
beat the boy mercilessly, often with froth on his mouth.
Then he would kiss his son passionately on the mouth,
reassuring him how much he loved him, which gave the boy
a melting feeling. It was this gratification which the boy—
and then the adult man—wanted to evoke through delin-
quent behavior. In his daily life, in his attitude toward his
family and his subordinates, he emulated the sadistic, try-
rannical father, while in his sexual behavior, that is, in
intercourse and anal masturbation, he identified with his
mother, fantasying being anally penetrated.

   In analysis, no technical device was able to make him
give up acting out the fantasy that by his perverse activities
he would arouse the anger of the analyst, which to him
meant being beaten. Any interpretation by the analyst was
used for gratification of his wish to be scolded and beaten;
silence was interpreted as the sullen response of the angered
father. His analysis seemed to have reached an impasse.

   His identification in his associations with Christ pun-
ished by God and thus achieving immortality finally elicited
the interpretation that through sexual fusion with the analyst
(father), he wanted to win protection against death. This

interpretation brought out a wealth of material hitherto withheld. "Death is and always was around me." He remembered having thought a lot about death as a child. "I have solved my fear of death through submission. . . . Being raped anally is protection against death." He resented that this had not been pointed out to him earlier.

His analysis took a similar course already, described in the foregoing (see pp. 105-106), and as elaborated in the following: He became depressed, felt constantly in a haze. "The analyst is dreaming interpretations," he said. Smoking, which was a substitute for masturbation and in which deep inhalation was especially meaningful, not only was incorporation of the foulsmelling mother, it also meant eating feces and thus "remaining a whole," immortal. The danger emanating from the respiratory incorporation of the hostile, "bad" mother in his smoking was undone by the subsequent punishment of being beaten, which was a regressive form of sexual fusion with the all-powerful father and simultaneously a prelude to it providing immortality. In gambling he not only was fed by an erratic but all-embracing mother, but also attempted to overcome his fear of nothingness by creating something out of nothing. Drinking meant oral gratification as well as ecstatic symbiotic fusion with his mother.

The working through of the transference as protection against death—he felt that as long as he was in analysis he would not die—led to the insight: "I have to accept fear of death." His subsequent depression led to a working through of his early symbiotic disturbance, and he finally succeeded in achieving a change in his behavior pattern. He developed feelings of love and tenderness toward his wife. His interest turned to the community. This basically bright man achieved a prominent position in his firm. At termination, the analysis could be regarded as relatively successful.

I shall in Chapter 5 comment further on the relationship between reparative mastery and depression. For now I should like to consider a treatment innovation that may shed light on the curative factors involved in the foregoing cases. I refer to the technique of "therapeutic playback," wherein analytic sessions are tape-recorded for later listening by the patient outside the consulting room. The interested reader should consult my earlier (1970) study for details of the technique and a consideration of its compatibility with standard analytic practice.

If it is not by now obvious, it is my view that the thought process of the neurotic—his test-acting in the mind—is inadequate. It operates insofar as he is neurotic, not in terms of his present potentialties, but in those of his infantile past. He responds to mature instinctual impulses in terms of his fixation to infantile ones. These infantile demands from within operate, as Freud (1940) expressed it, as traumata. There exists, therefore, persistence of, or regression to, not only repressed infantile wishes and conflicts in the id, but also to infantile ego function. The dependent infantile ego, fixated to infantile evaluation of danger, is pitted against the mature autonomous ego and restricts the latter in its operations. As a consequence, the patient suffers from an inadequacy of his adaptive ability, from deficiencies of reality functions and of object relations, and from lack of instinctual gratification. He functions on the fragile basis of pseudointegratedness.

Analysis purports to replace pseudointegratedness with a reality-syntonic integratedness. What has to be corrected is the deficiency in reality testing that, in itself preconscious and automatized, shapes actual behavior. Analysis can be called a transformation of pseudointegratedness into reality-syntonic integratedness based on reassessment of hitherto repressed inner processes. For this purpose, primal repression has to be lifted.

Freud saw the mainstay of the analytic process in the widening of consciousness – in making conscious repressed instinctual impulses and the defenses against them. The stress was on filling the gaps in remembering. The later structural slogan "where id was, there ego shall be (1933, p. 80)," deprived consciousness of its systemic meaning, but it did not alter the basic goal: "to bring into consciousness that which is unconscious no matter to which psychic institution it belongs" A. Freud (1936, p. 28).

The process of becoming conscious and its effect on behavior deserves more study in the light of ego psychology (Klein, 1965). It does not fully cover the complex and not yet completely clarified processes operating in the successful cure. It is indeed a remnant of the old cathartic theory, except that strangulated affect has been replaced by repressed impulse. Yet becoming conscious of an instinctual impulse, aggressive or libidinal, or of a defense – although undoubtedly an essential part of the curative process – seems not to be as automatically curative as would appear from Freud's writings.

Other investigations, stressing the role of ego function, have explored in more detail the inner psychic processes operating in the cure. Kris (1956) and Loewenstein (1956) have added to the classical goal of rendering conscious instinctual impulses that of gaining insight, which stresses the role of the synthesizing function of the ego. Loewenstein (1956) writes:

> Freud's original formulation of the aim of psychoanalytic therapy – to lift amnesias – was sufficient as long as only the undoing of the effects of repression was considered. But since psychoanalysis came to consider the results of other defensive mechanisms as well, the need has also arisen to encompass such processes as the re-establishment of connexions, for instance, and

the correction of distortions produced by various mechanisms of defense. We refer here to the important role of the synthetic and organizing function in the therapeutic process. Under these circumstances we are justified, I believe, in supplementing the term "bringing to consciousness" by the more comprehensive one "gaining of insight" when we wish to designate the results of changes in the ego which make warded-off mental functions available to the conflict-less sphere of the ego [pp. 460–461].

He adds, "Brought to consciousness [our psychic antiquities] become harmless because insight and verbalization subject them to reality-testing and thus unravel the effects of the pathogenic intertwinement between past and present" [p. 466]. In the latter formulation, insight is regarded as a precondition for reality testing. But is insight not, rather, the effect of testing? An examination of the relation between rendering conscious, achieving insight, and reality testing might clarify the therapeutic process. It will bring into focus the function of self-objectification, which can be regarded as the main road toward gaining insight.

Becoming conscious implies objectification, that is, awareness of an object, be it an outer or inner one, and simultaneously an awareness of the experiencing self distinct from the outer or inner environment. In becoming conscious there are variations not only in degree, focus, quality, and concreteness of awareness, but also in its objectivity, that is, its syntonicity with reality. Consciousness might be called every mode of awareness, even when there is only little differentiation between self and object representations; there might even be only a feeling of awareness devoid of discrete object and self representation. The focus of awareness might be on the object, it might be on the self. What comes to awareness may vary with regard to quality.

Awareness in any particular state of consciousness is seen as a light playing on dark waters, constantly subject to disciplining forces. The light can be bright or dim, sharply focused or vaguely diffused, and the experiences it produces vary qualitatively as images or perceptions or memories, etc.; the pattern of awareness and differences among them would describe the different states of consciousness [G. Klein, 1959, p. 18].

My concern here is with the varying degree not only of objectification but also of objectivity in the evaluation of the object. When Bibring (1937) wrote, "We subject the repressed instinctual impulses to an extensive interpretation . . . make them conscious and objectify them" (p. 176), he meant something different from Kris (1956), who listed among the functions involved in gaining insight "the ability of the ego to view the self and to observe its own functions with some measure of objectivity" (p. 450). The former refers to making the impulse into an object of investigation, the latter to being objective in this process. Both meanings are reflected in Webster's Third New International Dictionary (1986), where to objectify is defined as "to cause to become or to assume the character of an object; to render objective; to externalize. "To externalize," however, which means to give the status of external reality to that which is in the mind – the mechanism operative, for example, in projection – I would call faulty objectification. I prefer the term objectivation for correction or elimination of subjective elements in the objectification of inner or outer reality. This correction may be achieved through reobjectification under certain conditions, such as comparison with similar previous experiences, as in testing; or under the influence of newly emerging memories, as occurs in free association.

Faulty objectification and its correction through testing

start early, enforced by the need to avoid repetition of the biotraumatic frustration. In the wake of deprivations elicited by hallucinations of need gratification, the infant explores perceptions of gratification, whether they do or do not disappear through movements of the body or parts of it. In imaginary test-acting, an intended action is arrested and carried out in imagination; the observed response of the self is used to decide on the course of action to be followed. Another form of experimental acting in the mind—extremely important, yet seldom mentioned—is retrograde testing, or retrograde experimental acting. It occurs when an action has ended in failure; then a recall of this action is induced in order to investigate the reason for the unpleasant outcome. To investigate, for example, the reason for a stomach pain, I recall previous meals and the feelings accompanying them. The accent is, as in all thought processes, on observation and objectification of the self.

Objectification requires detachment from actual pressure for action. With increase of instinctual need, reality-syntonic awareness of the object, of its properties, movements, relations, is increasingly faulty. Faulty objectification is ubiquitous in infancy because of the overwhelming pressure for immediate need gratification. The same applies to the neurotic. His ego, as far as he is neurotic, is fixated in his reality testing, to infantile evaluation of needs and dangers, and thus to faulty objectification.

Prototypical situations for faulty objectification and its correction are, first, the instinctual interchange with the mother, appearing and disappearing, satisfying and depriving, benevolent and hostile; and, second, the child's investigation of the permanent object in his play activities.

The inevitable traumatic frustrations occurring in the child's instinctual interchange with the mother—unavoidable because of his immaturity at that phase—induce separation of self and non-self. Freud has pointed to faulty objectification in the early separation of the pleasure self from the unpleasure self. This separation is the effect of libidinization through trauma. In such a situation the unpleasure sensation is assumed to be projected to the outside and thus, separated from the self, will become the "bad" protoobject.

Another prototypical situation for both faulty objectification and its correction is the play activity of the child, remote from the urge for gratification of major instinctual needs. In his play, the child alternates between faulty objectification and its correction. By undoing magically the frustrations from the instinctual interchange with mother, his play becomes the source of faulty objectification. At the same time, the child in his play attempts realistic mastery of the permanent object and, observing the result of his attempts and repeating them, becomes increasingly aware of the distinction between self and object and the real qualities of both.

The need for correction of faulty objectification through retesting, built into the ego, is, together with instinctual frustration, one of the strongest of the patient's motivations. He comes into treatment because he wants to understand his failure in order to correct it. That the patient at the same time unconsciously expects this correction from the gratification of obsolete infantile needs, and therefore instigates a reenactment of the infantile situation, lays the ground for the antithetical aspect of the analytic process, which accounts for its success and also for its eventual failure.

In analysis, correction of faulty objectification occurs with the help of the analytic rule of free association. Free associations are verbalizations of derivatives of unconscious images and thoughts, fed by wishes for gratification of infantile needs, instinctual and self-preservative.

The analytic rule has antithetical effects as well, however. It allows the emergence of more and more derivatives of the primally repressed, as well as the reenactment of these in the transference neurosis. (Fantasies relived in attitudes, reactions, and even in behavior though limited by considerations of reality I call "reenactment," in contrast to "acting out," which disregards reality as, for example, in perversion.) The analytic "rule implies that the [patient's] ego suspends part of its censorship, can let a partial regression of its function carry on for a while and is able later to regain its grip" (Kris, 1956, p. 450). The ego suspends its censorship and then takes it up again; exclusion of reality testing is followed by its reinstatement. This antithetical effect of the analytic rule is possible through the multiple effect of verbalization, which enables the patient to use the analytic rule in the service of regression and, at the same time, in the service of the integrative function of the ego. By means of verbalization, psychic processes become objectified, objects and situations remote in space and time become accessible to manipulation. Yet verbalization may function also as communication, appeal, discharge in expression (Loewenstein, 1956, p. 462), imaginary magic gratification, and, of course, as action—either magical or realistic; we have only to think of insult, praise, seduction, or provocation.

The neurotic's proneness to use verbalization for magical wish fulfillment is especially significant. A patient reports: "Talking about something is like doing it; when I talk about my wish to sleep here I feel like going to sleep." Through the multiple function of verbalization, the patient's transference readiness will be transformed into the transference neurosis, that is, into reenactment of infantile situations. The specific state of consciousness in the session, induced by relative sensory deprivation, the transitory exclusion of reality testing and of action, brings this state of mind close to dreaming and, like the latter, facilitates the emergence of derivatives of the primally repressed.

Reenactment of infantile situations and their objectification in the transference neurosis sustain and complement each other. The analyst uses the memories emerging from the transference neurosis for its dissolution. Reenactment, however, has to remain a preparatory step. For the success of the analysis, objectification must prevail over reenactment. Only objectification by the autonomous ego enables the patient to dissolve the fixation to obsolete and faulty infantile self and object representations.

Gaining insight is not identical with integration. Only inclusion of insight into the automatic, preconscious thought processes that guide our actions achieves the change in action habits which we call integratedness. That insight is only a step toward integratedness is evidenced in the constant slipping back into the unconscious of insight laboriously gained in treatment. Kris (1952) explained this re-repression with incomplete integration, comparing it with similar lapses of memory in the process of problem solving. Only when in the therapeutic process the ego has completed its integrative function is insight protected against slipping from conscious awareness. Kris implies that this completion will be achieved by recapitulation in working through, which, as we know, occurs under greatly varying conditions, namely, under the influence of derivatives emerging from the unconscious, and hitherto repressed connections, and of various actual day residues—that is, under the influence of dynamic changes produced by the analytic process.

It is especially pertinent for our investigation that Kris assigns the ability to eliminate re-repression to the increase of self-observation in working through. Self-observation, in pitting one ego function against another, achieves its end by reestablishing links that have been lost. The dynamic factor in self-observation is, according to him, recognition. He assumes that through the perception involved, recognition leads to recall of the original situation: "Previously not sufficiently invested id derivatives can be integrated into the pattern indicated by the reconstruction; this [pattern] in turn strengthens the ego's position, permits a reduction of countercathexes and the gradual infiltration of further material . . ." (Kris, 1952, p. 309).

This is all the more important inasmuch as the final success of working through depends on the strength of the ego, that is, on the strength and nature of its fixation and of the anxiety associated with it. The patient, for fear of changing horses in midstream, may cling to pseudointegratedness because of its seemingly proven utility and predictability. Thus the apparent stability of dispositions to repeat efforts at reparative mastery. In these instances, working through all too often will not achieve completion of integration, but rather will be used for ceaseless reenactment of infantile dependency. In these instances analysis deteriorates to a new edition of the disease it is supposed to cure.

What determines the outcome is the ratio between the strength of the mature ego and that of the dependent infantile part. Where the infantile ego prevails, the patient clings to infantile dependency, to faulty objectification and the illusions it engenders of gratification of infantile needs, including the need for protection against any danger, even death. Everything, therefore, that weakens the prevalence of the infantile ego or strengthens the function of the autonomous ego will tip the balance in favor of cure.

By increasing self-objectification and creating a climate better suited for correction of faulty objectification, playback achieves both. The analytic procedure conducive to regressive reenactment is not unconditionally favorable to achieving the desired objectification and integration. The recumbent position, the invisibility of the analyst, the fundamental rule, the analyst's behavior—all these increase the trend toward regression and produce an emotional climate that significantly limits the patient's ability for self-objectivation. This explains why final relinquishment of the neurosis may occur only after termination of analysis. Some patients who suffered, for example, from impotence became fully potent only several months after termination of their analyses. The playback technique succeeds in balancing these disadvantages. It increases working through under conditions that facilitate objectification: As the patient re-listens, the session will be recapitulated; in a subsequent session, the response to relistening may emerge directly, or in free associations, or in dreams; all this will, in turn, be listened to at home. The steady, persistent alternation con-stitutes unrelenting working through. "It hangs on and on," as a patient remarked. Thus, playback assigns working through to an intramural as well as an extramural locality: first, to the analytic session, which, through its permissive-ness, is relatively exempt from the inexorable laws governing reality but for precisely this reason instigates the reenact-ment of fantasies arising from the infantile child-parent dependency; second, to the playback, which, being remote from the impact of the direct transference dependency, favors the objectification of the latter. This separation repeats the separation of the child at play from the direct impact of the instinctual interchange with his mother. The advantage of such a separation seems to have been recognized by Freud and other analysts (e.g., Federn) when they encouraged patients to keep diaries and records of their analyses, espe-cially of their dreams, after the session. Many patients stress that the separation creates a mental climate better suited to the integration of the analyst's interpretations. One patient remarked, "It's hard for me to listen to you here. It's easier to listen to what you say at home." Another said, "I am too full of emotions while talking here. When I listen to myself at home, it becomes more vital to me, as if someone else had given me a tape to listen to. Here it's difficult to listen to me. I am too much concerned with what I am telling you."

Through relistening, the split between the infantile ego,

reenacting, and the mature ego, objectifying (A. Freud, 1965; Sterba, 1934), becomes more pronounced. The objectifying function of listening to one's own voice while talking (Klein, 1965) is doubled. Freed from the dangers that the emergence of infantile instinctual needs in the analytic situation carry with it, the patient is better able to become aware of his resistance, his defenses, the distortions created by anxiety, guilt, shame, and the wish to please.

> When I listened, I became aware of anxiety I had not felt in the session. That I chose my words carefully so as not to offend you. I heard myself carefully beat around the bush. I was talking as if I was dealing with a highly unstable person—with a person who would not listen through, but would smack me immediately. I became aware of the terror and my fear of you. I was treating you as I did my mother.

Objectification thus leads by way of reality testing to correction of judgments about inner and outer reality and thus to insight.

Bibring (1937) has pointed out that through objectification the pleasurable character of latent instinctual gratification is at first brought out and relived, "gradually lessened, subjected to criticism intermixed with unpleasure and finally completely dispelled" (p. 176). The control of acting out of irrational transference affects puts the interpersonal exchange between analyst and patient on a more realistic basis.

> With the tape I listened as a third party. I could not do this before the tape. When you talked, I only heard the edge, the threat, the criticism, and was angry. On the tape, I heard your great authentic effort to listen, to understand, and to communicate. I was not used to this, and I transferred it back to the session.

The increase of self objectification in relistening interferes with uninhibited reenactment of infantile situations;
mature autonomous ego function replaces the infantile superego. A patient reports:

> I feel that when I listen to me on the tape, that this is
> an impossible person. It makes me crazy, again and
> again the little boy wailing. I must admit that your silly
> tapes had an effect on me.
>
> It nauseates me greatly, when I listen to this imma-
> ture guy talking about wanting to get enemas. . . . It's
> disgusting. I develop a hate of myself. My veneer is
> shattered, which protected me in analysis. I don't like
> that.
>
> I feel like a slob at all that talking about eating. I like
> to escape, but I know damned well I can't. I can't be
> any more that self-centered conceited person. It is
> unpleasant to contemplate me. I see myself—the
> whole battle to wean away from mother. Sometimes I
> forgot that I am an adult who is no longer a kid.

In childhood the infantile superego, built on introjection
of specific aspects of the parental objects, is gradually
relinquished and merges with the maturing ego. In treatment, the maturing of infantile parts of the ego parallels this
development. In the beginning, the patient certainly adds
his analyst's image to the introjected objects. In the course of
analysis, however, objectivation and genetic reduction—in
concurrence with the consistently benevolent and helpful
attitude of the analyst—effect further maturation of the ego
and a dissolution of the infantile dependency (Bibring, 1937;
Jacobson, 1964). The infantile superego partially merges with
the maturing ego (Strachey, 1934; Kris, 1956; Jacobson,
1964), partially it becomes the receptor of group demands.
Infantile obedience to the superego turns into consistent,

infantile superego, with automatic self-evaluation. The patient learns to act on the basis of his independent ego functions, though under the shadow of group demands. This is of course a circular process. Increasing extension of the mature ego brings to bear present potentialities and values on self-evaluation. This process is significantly strengthened by the increase of self-objectification in the playback, which fosters the shift from passive dependence, from the wish for the analyst's love and protection (or rebellion against it), to a more rational working alliance. The patient becomes able to tune in more effectively with the analyst and with the goal of the analytic process. One patient expressed this nicely:

> Before [the introduction of the playback] there was only me who was not caring what I did or saw in the session. Now there are two me's—one is doing analysis and the other is an observer who sees the childish behavior in it and suffers. I see a lot of things I didn't think of before.
>
> The tapes put a burden on me. I have to work much harder; it shifts the task to me. I feel it's tremendously beneficial for me. I do the hard work. I go throught it again and again. I feel I can do the work myself. I don't need you.
>
> When I listen to the tape I become the analyst. I am playing your role. I get a feeling of my own strength when I do it.
>
> It's hopeful that I am able to find out something from the tape even when it is devastating. I now show more aggression toward you, but I have a positive feeling "I can do it." It makes me feel grown-up.

5

The Teleonomic Principle

In Chapter 1 I proposed that pavor nocturnus be viewed as a physiological defense against stress resulting from a preceding nightmare. I demonstrated the compatibility of the alternating phases of inhibition and excitation observed therein with Selye's conception of countershock and suggested that anxiety is associated at first with an inhibition of physiological activity serving a signal function. In Chapter 3 I argued that the repetitive character of such dreams demonstrates a failure of mastery, which is to say, a failure in the psychological mechanism we describe in the concept signal anxiety. This failure was conceived in developmental terms as a failure to attribute meaning to one's own states of tension, and was viewed as operative in the repetitive phenomena of the transference neurosis as well as in pavor nocturnus. These repetitive phenomena were elaborated in

139

Chapter 4 in terms of the meaningless renunciations of subjectivity represented by reparative mastery of inadequately developed ego functions and were laid to experiences of traumatization in the symbiotic phase of development. I suggested that depression invariably followed the interpretation of reparative mastery in treatment.

I should now like to propose (1) that the state of tension to which meaning is not attributed in the transference neurosis is precisely the inhibition of physiological activity observed in pavor nocturnus, and (2) that this state of primary physiological depression is itself the depression observed upon interpretation of reparative mastery in treatment. Obviously, my formulation departs from classical energy theory under which it is impossible to conceive of an inhibition of physiological activity as a state of tension. Inasmuch as it is derived from homeostatic theory, it characterizes tension in terms of disequilibrium or disorganization of somatic functions. It also departs from our usual conceptions of anxiety as response to trauma, and depression as response to loss of object. Depression, as much as subsequent agitation, is the anxious response to trauma *because* the unmastered state of tension to which trauma gave rise—the depression itself—cannot be displaced to the danger of separation from the symbiotic object. The need for the symbiotic object is as subjectively alien to the patient as the physiological state to which it responds. That is why, for example, the interpretation of transference as an irrational protection against death leads to depression. It confronts the patient with the inevitability of separating from the analyst, because it addresses what is subjectively alien to him. When patients subsequently verbalize their fantasies of symbiotic union with the analyst, it becomes possible for them, with the assistance of the analyst, to recognize objectively their reliance on that assistance. In effect, the analyst performs the functions of the original good-enough mother in the development of objectivation in the face of tension. Thus it is only when primary depression can be utilized as a *psychological* signal of anxiety that we can speak of depression as the result of loss of object.

It is interesting in this regard that in at least one instance Freud (1923) seemed to equate the processes involved in automatic anxiety and depression:

> Fear of death, *Todesangst*, [mortal terror] makes its appearance under two conditions (which, moreover, are entirely analogous to situations in which other kinds of anxiety develop), namely, as a reaction to an external danger and as an internal process, as for instance in melancholia. . . . The fear of death in melancholia only admits of one explanation: that the ego gives itself up because it feels itself hated and persecuted by the super-ego, instead of loved. To the ego, therefore, living means the same as being loved. . . . But, when the ego finds itself in an excessive real danger which it believes itself unable to overcome by its own strength, it is bound to draw the same conclusion. It sees itself deserted by all protecting forces and lets itself die. Here, moreover, is once again the same situation as that which underlay the first great anxiety-state of birth and the infantile anxiety of longing—the anxiety due to separation from the protecting mother [p. 58].

The differences between this formulation and my own should be apparent: I regard the ego as insufficienty developed to be "given up" in the situation of tension; and I believe that primary depression is operative in all biotraumatic situations and that it reappears as a signal—in an attenuated way—in all forms of psychic depression. The "general enfeeblement and disturbance of the mental capacities" to which Freud referred in *Beyond the Pleasure Principle* corresponds to the phase of primary depression, which *follows* the agitation phase in the countershock defense.

I believe we may now consider the larger issues that this formulation faces in terms of Monod's (1971) teleonomic theory of evolution, wherein, by virtue of the autonomous morphogenesis and invariant reproduction characteristic of all living beings, chance occurrences become necessities. Those necessities—and, more important, the qualities of invariant reproduction and autonomous morphogenesis from which they derive—explain the goal-directed, or "teleonomic," character of life. Since it is individual human development with which we are concerned, let us consider the repetition of traumatic events in dreams and treatment in the light of Monod's conception of autonomous morphogenesis: A living being's structure results from a process that

> it owes almost nothing to the action of outside forces, but everything, from its overall shape down to its tiniest detail, to "morphogenetic" interactions within the object itself. It is thus a structure giving proof of an autonomous determinism: precise, rigorous, implying a virtually total "freedom" with respect to outside agents or conditions—which are capable, to be sure, of impeding this development, but not of governing or guiding it, not of prescribing its organizational scheme to the living object [pp. 10–11].

In effect, man's nature generates itself. And this self-generating quality extends even to behavior man acquires through experience:

> Certain contemporary ethologists still seem attached to the idea that the elements of animal behavior are some of them innate, some learned, the one mode of

acquisition being strictly separate from and absolutely excluding the other. How completely mistaken this conception is has been vigorously demonstrated by Lorenz. When behavior implies elements acquired through experience, they are acquired according to a *program*, and that program is innate—that is to say, genetically determined. The program's structure initiates and guides early learning, which will follow a certain preestablished pattern defined in the species' genetic patrimony [pp. 152-153].

Monod is arguing, then, that the program according to which behavior is acquired through experience is as much a "structure" characterized by autonomous morphogenesis as is the organism's "overall shape." And, as we have seen, the development of such structures, which "owes almost nothing to the action of outside forces," is yet capable of being "impeded" by those forces, that is to say, by experience. By implication, behavior cannot be acquired through experience which impedes the development of the structure that "initiates and guides" its acquisition.

Monod conceives of such development in terms of information: "All teleonomic structures and performances can be regarded as corresponding to a certain quantity of information which must be transmitted for these structures to be realized and these performances accomplished" (p. 14). By that token, when the program that guides early learning is prevented from being "realized," is impeded by "outside conditions," then those conditions can be conceived as preventing the "transmission" of information necessary for development. Monod means more here than the infliction of neural injury. Obviously, behavior acquired through experience cannot be acquired in its absence, without information provided or represented by outside conditions. It follows, then, that the program cannot be realized, that the performance of learning cannot be accomplished in the face of outside conditions that prevent the transmission of necessary experience. It is on this basis, I believe, that we must conceive trauma, as the result of a lack of information necessary to the accomplishment of a developmentally functional performance. If the performance is the maintenance of homeostatic equilibrium in the very young infant, then the "missing" information can be conceptualized (among other ways) as the lack of the "holding and soothing" presence of the mother who vouchsafes that equilibrium. So, too, would a lack of verbal stimulation, for example, constitute the "missing" information necessary to the performance functionally antecedent to the development of language.

This formulation places certain constraints on how we conceptualize the development of mastery. No matter how many times the traumatic event is repeated in memory, its repetition cannot generate the information necessary for its mastery, since the only possible source of that information is the genetic program itself, the development of which is impeded by trauma. The human surround can supply or represent the information necessary for the avoidance of trauma, but it cannot "govern or guide" the development of the program, cannot "prescribe its organizational scheme to the living object." Mastery, in sum, cannot be acquired from the human surround. Nor can it be generated by the developmentally arrested program. The traumatic event is repeated not *in order* to be mastered, but because it is the nature of the performance to remember.

In *Beyond the Pleasure Principle* Freud acknowledged his preference for maintaining the dualism of his theoretical system and, by implication, his preference for preserving conflict as the basis for individual development in psychoanalytic theory. Thus the opposition between the urge to restore an earlier state of things—the death instinct—and the life instinct. But no matter Freud's reluctance to regard as an instinct the "more instinctual" compulsion to repeat, and no matter at what remove he placed it from the death instinct, the gist of his argument in *Beyond the Pleasure Principle* is that the child incapable of mastery is compelled by his nature— his developmentally "more primitive" nature (attributed in not so many words to the death instinct)—to repeat the traumatic event in memory; the rise in tension resulting from this assertion of his nature necessarily implied as well an "opposing nature" (the life instinct); this conflict within the organism itself was thus the necessary, if not sufficient, condition for the development of mastery. On the basis of my foregoing formulation, however, this conception can no longer be viewed as tenable: Truly it is man's nature to generate itself; but it is not his nature to generate its opposite. This, I believe, is a most powerful argument in favor of contemporary, conflict-free conceptions of ego development, and the reason why I stressed earlier that subjective attribution of meaning is the precondition for conflict.

The self-generating character of human nature is all the more difficult for us to comprehend in the light of the advent of subjectivity and anticipation in individual development. The attribution of meaning to the external event seems to bridge the unbridgeable divide called for by teleonomic theory. But although man is programmed to attribute meaning to the event, that meaning cannot alter the program itself; it cannot create a new, structurally different form of knowing in the individual, a new performance beyond what Monod calls "subjective simulation." And although it is true that such meaning may create conditions favorable for the selection of an altered program in the mutations of future generations—Monod acknowledges the paramount significance of culture at the present stage of human evolution—it cannot change the direction of development in the individual organism itself.

And yet there does seem to be something "necessary"

about the experience of trauma for human development. Unlike lower species, man is born with relatively few inherited patterns of behavior. At birth, and even soon after, the development of ganglion cells in every part of the brain is incomplete. That incompleteness of development is much more pronounced in the human infant than in any other mammalian young. Moreover, the growth of the brain after birth does not consist, as does that of other tissues and organs, in the multiplication of its cells. The increase in the brain is exclusively the result of growth of fibers and arborizations that spread out from developing cells, establishing the potential for various connections. The fixed patterns of innate instinctual action in lower species are thus replaced in man by the potential for innumerable responses based on the wealth of associative fibers in the brain. That is why, for instance, the quicker maturation of monkeys' brains – of pathways for fixed action patterns – makes them less amenable to learning than is man. Man's capacity for anticipation, then, appears to require the immaturity of his brain at birth. And that same immaturity accounts for his dependence on the human surround for protection against trauma.

Is trauma, then, necessary for individual development? The answer is clearly no. But it is equally clear that the inevitable experience of trauma was *absolutely necessary* to the development of an innate program capable of generating anticipation. As Monod puts it:

> Everything comes from experience; yet not from ongoing current experience, reiterated by each individual with each new generation, but instead, from the experiences accumulated by the entire ancestry of the species over the course of its evolution. Only this experience wrung from chance – only those countless trials chastened by selection – could, as with any other

organ, have made the central nervous system into an organ adapted to its particular function [p. 154].

I need only add that in that "vast and bitter experience of our humble ancestors" (p. 158) the function of the nervous system in producing a physiological defense against shock must have been paramount. And that the function of that defense remains paramount today in providing a signal, in the form of agitated behavior to the human surround and in the form of primary depression to the individual, of the need for external assistance in the face of disorganizing states of tension.

Let it be said, finally, that we are no closer today to an understanding of the development of subjectivity and anticipation in man than was Freud. At the very least, however, I believe that our psychoanalytic investigations must be guided by the considerations I have addressed herein, as to the physiology of stress and the teleonomic character of human evolution.

References

Baruk, H. (1949), Experimental catatonia and the problem of will and personality. *J. Nerv. Ment. Dis.*, 110:218–235.

Bibring, E. (1937), Symposium on the theory of therapeutic results in psycho-analysis. *Internat. J. Psycho-Anal.*, 18:170–189.

Broughton, R. (1968), Sleep disorders: Disorders of arousal? *Science*, 159:170–189.

Fisher, C., Byrne, J., Edwards, A. & Kahn, E. (1970), A psychophysiological study of nightmares. *J. Amer. Psychoanal. Assn.*, 18:747–782.

_____ Kahn, E., Edwards, A. & Davis, D. (1974a), A psychophysiological study of nightmares and night terrors. I. Physiological aspects of the Stage 4 night terrors. *Psychoanal. & Contemp. Sci.*, 3:317–398.

_____ Fine, J. (1974b), A psychophysiological study of the nightmares and night terrors. *J. Nerv. & Ment. Dis.*, 158:174–188.

Freud, A. (1936), *The Ego and the Mechanisms of Defense*. New York: International Universities Press, 1966.

_____ (1960), Discussion of Dr. John Bowlby's paper. *The Psycho-*

151

analytic Study of the Child, 15:53–62. New York: International Universities Press.

———— (1965), *Normality and Pathology in Childhood*. New York: International Universities Press.

Freud, S. (1895), On the grounds for detaching a particular syndrome from neurathenia under the description "anxiety" neurosis. *Standard Edition*, 3:90–115. London: Hogarth Press, 1962.

———— (1900), *The Interpretation of Dreams. Standard Edition*, 4 & 5. London: Hogarth Press, 1953.

———— (1905), Three essays on the theory of sexuality. *Standard Edition*, 7:133–243. London: Hogarth Press, 1953.

———— (1920), *Beyond the Pleasure Principle. Standard Edition*, 18:7–64. London: Hogarth Press, 1955.

———— (1923), The ego and the id. *Standard Edition*, 19:13–66. London: Hogarth Press, 1961.

———— (1925), An autobiographical study. *Standard Edition*, 20:7–70. London: Hogarth Press, 1959.

———— (1926), Inhibitions, symptoms, and anxiety. *Standard Edition*, 20:87–172. London: Hogarth Press, 1959.

———— (1933), New introductory lectures on psycho-analysis. *Standard Edition*, 22:57–81. London: Hogarth Press, 1964.

———— (1940), An outline of psycho-analysis. *Standard Edition*, 23:144–207. London: Hogarth Press, 1964.

Gastaut, H. & Broughton, R. (1965), A clinical and polygraphic study of episodic phenomena during sleep. In: *Recent Advances in Biological Psychiatry*, Vol. 7, ed. J. Wortis. New York: Plenum, pp. 197–221.

Harlow, F. & Harlow, M. (1965), Total social isolation effects on Macaque Monkey behavior. *Science*, 14:666.

Holt, R. (1967), The development of the primary process: A structural view. In: *Motives and Thought: Psychoanalytic Essays in Honor of David Rapaport. Psychological Issues* (Monogr. 18/19), ed. R. Holt. New York: International Universities Press.

Jacobson, E. (1964), *The Self and the Object World*. New York: International Universities Press.

Jones, E. (1931), *On the Nightmare*. London: Hogarth Press.

de Jong, H. (1945), *Experimental Catatonia*. Baltimore, MD: Williams & Wilkins.

Klein, G. (1959), Consciousness in psychoanalytic theory. *J. Amer. Psychoanal. Assn.*, 7:5–34.

_____ (1965), On hearing one's own voice: An aspect of cognitive control in spoken thought. In: *Psychoanalytic and Current Biological Thought*, ed. H. Greenfield & W. Lewis. Madison: University of Wisconsin Press, pp. 245–273.

Kris, E. (1952), *Psychoanalytic Explorations in Art*. New York: International Universities Press.

_____ (1956), On some vicissitudes of insight in psychoanalysis. *Internat. J. Psycho-Anal.*, 37:445–455.

Loewenstein, R. M. (1956), Some remarks on the role of speech in psycho-analytic technique. *Internat. J. Psycho-Anal.*, 37: 460–468.

Mack, J. E. (1965), Nightmares, conflict and ego development in childhood. *Internat. J. Psycho-Anal.*, 46:403–428.

_____ (1970), *Nightmares and Human Conflict*. Boston, MA: Little, Brown.

Monod, J. E. (1971), *Chance and Necessity*. New York: Vintage, 1972.

Moon, V. (1942), *Shock*. Philadelphia: Lea & Febiger.

Panel (1968), A. F. Valenstein (chairman). Psychoanalytic theory of instinctual drives in relation to recent developments, H. Dahl reporter. *J. Amer. Psychoanal. Assn.*, 16:613–637.

Rapaport, D. (1960), Psychoanalysis as a developmental psychology. *Collected Papers*, ed. M. Gill. New York: Basic, 1967, pp. 820–852.

Rechtschaffen, A., Vogel, G. & Sheikun, G. (1963), Interrelatedness of mental activity during sleep. *Arch. Gen. Psychiat.*, 9:536–547.

Ribble, M. (1939), Significance of infantile sucking for psychic development. *J. Nerv. Ment. Dis.*, 90:455–463.

_____ (1941), Disorganizing factors of infant personality. *Amer. J. Psychiat.*, 98:459–463.

Roffwarg, H. P., Muzio, J. N. & Dement, W. C. (1966), Ontogenetic development of the human sleep-dream cycle. *Science*, 152:604–619.

Schrödinger, E. (1945), *What is Life? Physical Aspects of the Living Cell*. Cambridge, Eng.: At the University Press.

Schur, H. (1969), Hallucinations in children. In: *The Unconscious Today: Essays in Honor of Max Schur*, ed. M. Kanzer. New York: International Universities Press, pp. 306–330.

Schur, M. (1958), The ego and the id in anxiety. *The Psychoanalytic Study of the Child*, 13:190–220. New York: International Universities Press.

Author Index

Subject Index